Hitler's Heroes During the Soviet Advance

Knight's Cross Generals on the Eastern Front, 3 February 1943–12 February 1944

Jeremy Dixon

FRONTLINE BOOKS

First published in Great Britain in 2025 by
Frontline Books
An imprint of Pen & Sword Books Limited
Yorkshire – Philadelphia

ISBN 978 1 03610 270 8

A CIP catalogue record for this book is
available from the British Library.

Typeset by Mac Style
Printed in the UK by CPI Group (UK) Ltd, Croydon, CR0 4YY.

The Publisher's authorised representative in the EU for product
safety is Authorised Rep Compliance Ltd., Ground Floor,
71 Lower Baggot Street, Dublin D02 P593, Ireland.
www.arccompliance.com

For a complete list of Pen & Sword titles please contact

PEN & SWORD BOOKS LIMITED
47 Church Street, Barnsley, South Yorkshire, S70 2AS, England
E-mail: enquiries@pen-and-sword.co.uk
Website: www.pen-and-sword.co.uk
or
PEN AND SWORD BOOKS
1950 Lawrence Road, Havertown, PA 19083, USA
E-mail: uspen-and-sword@casematepublishers.com
Website: www.penandswordbooks.com

Hitler's Heroes During the Soviet Advance

Dedicated to Ann Driscoll

Contents

Acknowledgements

I would like to thank Paul Budden for his valuable advice and his continued support as well as proof reading this book. I must also thank my mum and dad, sister and nephews, for their support, as well as my friends: Ann Driscoll, Jo Robinson, Jo Jeffrey, Emily Budgen, Jane Budgen, Angela Axton-Green, Nick Isles, Hazel Kirby, Jackie Snowling, Tracy Dover, Carol Ryan, Nicola Willoughby, Lisa Hunt, Josie Hobson, Bev Drew, Kelly Delroy, Vanessa Gardner, Lauretta Kelly, Daniella Craig, Janet Baklish, Jane Ramsey, Linda Hurd, Colin Harris, Alex Curran, Nathan Pearce, Debra and Dave Mills.

Introduction

This is the third of a four-volume work that describes how German officers who held the rank of General won the highest award for bravery, the Knight's Cross. This third volume describes how the 116 generals: (two Generaloberst; nineteen full-generals; fifty-three Generalleutnants and forty-two Generalmajors) won their Knight's Cross and higher grades during the Soviet campaign.

On 3 February 1943 Berlin acknowledged the end of the fighting in Stalingrad, with German radio stating, 'the sacrifices of the Army, bulwark of a historical European mission, were not in vain'. Germany began a three-day period of national mourning. The following day Soviet forces landed on the Black Sea coast near Novorossiysk ready to destroy the trapped forces of German Army Group A. The German 6th Army had suffered at least 300,000 dead or wounded with

Friedrich Paulus.

Walter Heitz.

Karl Eibl.   Karl Strecker [right] with Carl Rodenburg.

another 91,000 taken prisoner, which included more than twenty generals and 2,000 officers (only 6,000 men would ever see Germany again). The *Luftwaffe* lost 488 aircraft and 1,000 air crews during the Stalingrad airlift.

The German generals captured at Stalingrad included the commander of the 6th Army, *Generalfeldmarschall* Friedrich Paulus, *Generaloberst* Walter

Walther von Seydlitz-Kurzbach.   Günther Angern.

Heitz, *General der Infanterie* Karl Eibl and Karl Strecker and *General der Artillerie* Walther von Seydlitz-Kurzbach. At least another five were killed at Stalingrad, which included *Generalleutnant* Günther Angern and *General der Infanterie* Alexander von Hartmann.

By 6 February Red Army forces had tightened their grip as they reached the Sea of Azov and were now within 5 miles of Rostov. The next day the Soviets announced complete control over the south bank of the Don River, which was recaptured on 8 February. Kursk, which had been held by the Germans since November 1941, was reoccupied by Soviet forces. The next day Soviet forces recaptured Belgorod and began to advance towards Kharkov. By the

Alexander von Hartmann.

12th, the escape route for the Germans from Rostov had been narrowed as the Soviets cut the main rail line at Krasnoarmeisk and Soviet forces threatened encirclement of the German forces defending Kharkov.

On 14 February Soviet forces recaptured Rostov, the main outlet for German forces retreating from the Caucasus. *Generalfeldmarschall* Ewald von Kleist's Army Group A had to withdraw to the Taman Peninsula between the Sea of Azov and the Black Sea. The First Panzer Army under *General der Kavallerie* Eberhard von Mackensen was the only German unit to get through to the north before Rostov fell. Two days later Kharkov was reoccupied by Soviet forces. Hitler equated its loss to Stalingrad and promised to retake Russia's fourth largest city. The Soviet army had by now advanced a total of 375 miles west of Stalingrad. On 19 February the Soviet 6th Army advanced to within 30 miles of *Generalfeldmarschall* Erich von Manstein's headquarters at Zaporozhye, which Hitler was visiting at the time. However, the Soviet advance ran out of fuel and was later knocked out by a German counter-attack. Hitler flew back to Germany to give Manstein a free hand to launch his counter-offensive. Later Manstein unleashed his attack, leaving the Soviet 6th Army shattered at Zmiyev. Both Soviet and German forces made up ground with the 4th Panzer Army under *Generaloberst* Hermann Hoth advancing on Pavlograd, with the the XXX. Army Corps under *General der Artillerie* Maximilian Fretter-Pico. They attacked Krasnoarmeyskaya and the 1st Panzer Army advanced towards Izyum, with the *Luftwaffe* flying 1,145 missions in support of Manstein's forces. On 25 February

Ewald von Kleist.

Eberhard von Mackensen.

Erich von Manstein.

Hermann Hoth, right, and Georg Pfeiffer.

Army Group Centre pulled out of the Rzhev salient with the Soviet Central Front joining the Bryansk Front, attacking German forces in the salient, and three days later the last German units left the Demjansk salient. Manstein's offensive had inflicted losses on the Soviets, killing 23,000 and capturing 9,000, plus destroying or capturing sixty-five tanks and 350 artillery pieces. On 2 March the German base at Rzhev was evacuated by Army Group Centre and the following day Soviet forces reoccupied Rzhev. German forces reached Kharkov on 11 March in a counter-attack that was described as a brilliant tactical move by Manstein, commander of Army Group South.

Maximilian Fretter-Pico.

On 16 March the Red Army recaptured Cholm after long battles and two days later the spring thaw halted all major operations. A week later the Soviet Rzhev–Vyazma Operations came to an end, with the Red Army having lost 38,862 killed or missing and 99,715 wounded. Following the end of Manstein's attack in the south on 9 April, the Red Army held a huge salient in the central sector of the front that bulged into German-held territory, the Kursk salient. On 14 April Hitler issued Operational Order No. 6 for the destruction of enemy forces in the Kursk salient. Hitler realised that 1943 was his last chance to avoid defeat in the East, a position made more urgent by the impending defeat of Axis forces in North Africa and U-boat losses in the Atlantic and with the threat of an Allied invasion of Western Europe. In early May, the Red Army halted a major German counteroffensive in the Kuban area. Then in early June, Red Air Force aircraft attacked German rear communications and airfields at Smolensk, Orel and Bryansk.

On 4 July the Germans launched Operation Citadel, which became the Battle of Kursk and involved the 9th Army under *Generaloberst* Walter Model with 335,000 men, 590 tanks and 424 assault guns, made up of thirty-two German divisions. On 5 July the Battle of Kursk began when the 9th Army attacked the Soviet 13th and 48th armies. The Germans, however, initially advanced no more than 1.2 miles towards their objective and by the evening they had advanced 6 miles but had sustained 20 per cent losses. Some 200 out of 300 tanks and numerous assault guns had been committed and the attackers had suffered 20,000 casualties. By the end of the day German forces had advanced almost 16 miles and were now involved in heavy fighting. In the south, the Germans flew 200 ground-attack missions in support of their ground troops but despite eight attacks by the panzer units they could not break through the Soviet lines. By 10 July it was clear that German success hinged on the 4th Panzer Army, and so the next day *Generaloberst* Model committed the 10th Panzer Grenadier Division and launched a series of desperate attacks on Ponyri. Although the Germans held most of the town, it was impossible for them to move as their losses had been so great. The Soviets stopped the Germans from breaking through at Kursk in the south and by 12 July the Germans had destroyed 192 Soviet tanks for the loss of only thirty of their own. As the tank battle raged on, 100 Soviet tanks broke through the German positions and the Red Army continued to push forward with 170,000 troops and more than 350 tanks. By the end of the day the Soviets had pushed 7 miles into the German lines, and a few days later the Soviet 3rd Guards Tank Army joined the offensive east of Orel in an effort to secure a link with Leningrad.

On 3 August the Soviet Operation Rumyanstev began with its objective the complete destruction of both the 4th Panzer Army and the 6th Army. The Voronezh and Steppe Fronts had more than 980,000 troops, 2,439 tanks, 12,627 guns and mortars and almost 1,300 aircraft. The offensive began and by early afternoon the German lines had been penetrated sufficiently for a Soviet attack. By 4 August the Red Army had driven a six-mile wedge between the 4th Army and Army Detachment *Kempf*. The following day the Soviets recaptured Orel and on the 7th the Soviets began their offensive to recapture Smolensk. They were joined by another 428,000 troops and attacked the German 3rd and 4th Panzer Armies, with the Germans losing 5,000 troops either killed or captured during their retreat. By the 15th the Soviet Southern Front had opened an offensive along the River Mius against the German 6th Army, and in Kharkov the German defenders resisted the sledgehammer blows of the Steppe Front.

On 23 August the Germans withdrew from Kharkov and two days later the Red Army began another offensive as they attacked the German 2nd Army. The Germans had no reserves and the Soviets were now threatening to split Army Groups Centre and South. Over the next few days the German front began to split. At the end of August the German 6th and 16th

Walter Model.

Armies prepared to fall back to the Dnieper, as Manstein finally managed to convince Hitler of the need for mobile defence. The Soviet armies showed no sign of halting and continued to push the Germans out of their country as they began to evacuate their forces west into the Crimea. On 14 September, as the German 9th Army pulled back from Bryansk, fighting with Soviet forces erupted in and around the city. A week later the Soviet front reached the River Dnieper but the cost was huge. The Soviets lost 40,000 killed and missing, with another 117,000 wounded. By 24 September Smolensk was virtually surrounded and the Germans were forced to abandon the city, which was occupied by the Soviets the next day. By the end of the month the Germans had retreated behind the Dnieper, and the Red Army had once again achieved a great success, liberating many towns and inflicting losses of 230,000 on the Germans. Army Group South had by now completed its evacuation of 200,000 wounded soldiers. During the next few days the Soviet army forced its way across the Dnieper, capturing Nevel, which cut all communications between German Army Groups North and Centre. By the 23rd the German 6th Army had retreated from Melitopol to the Dnieper and this left the 17th Army isolated in the Crimea. By the beginning of November the Soviet offensive to liberate Kiev had begun and the 4th Panzer Army had suffered heavy casualties. On 15 November Manstein counter-attacked from the southern base of the Soviet salient, his aim being to take Kiev. Two days later, with his counter-attack in full swing, his XXXXVIII. Panzer Corps captured Zhitomir. The Soviets responded and Manstein had to withdraw in the face of superior numbers, with his forces grinding to a halt short of Kiev.

On 30 November Manstein launched a fresh attack in the Zhitomir area, and the German LIX. Army Corps recaptured Korosten from the Soviet 16th Army. On 8 December the XXXXVIII. Panzer Corps reached the River Teterev but was slowed by enemy resistance, a few days later it became apparent that there were more Red Army units in the area than the Germans originally believed. By the 23rd the German panzer corps had halted its attacks in the face of superior enemy forces and a few days later the Soviet 60th Army captured Korosten and cut off Zhitomir, trapping the German XIII. Army Corps. On 5 January 1944 the Soviets opened their offensive against the German 8th Army and began a tough fight near Kirovograd. Fierce fighting took place in many areas over the next few days and by the 14th a new offensive around Leningrad began as the Soviets began to free the city from the Germans. On 17 January the German Army Group commander, *Generalfeldmarschall* Georg von Küchler, committed his reserves of three infantry divisions against the 8th Army at Mga. Two days later the Soviet 2nd Shock and 42nd Armies linked up at Ropsha, which meant the end of the Leningrad siege. On 21 January Novgorod was captured

Georg von Küchler.   Karl-Adolf Hollidt.

by the Soviets and a week later the Soviet 54th Army captured Lyuban and *Feldmarschall* Küchler ordered a retreat to the River Luga to save his Army Group. The following day Hitler replaced Küchler with *Generaloberst* Walter Model.

On 30 January the German 6th Army was attacked by the 3rd and 4th Ukrainian Fronts and fighting began near the Nikopol bridgehead. The Soviets had 257,000 troops and 1,400 tanks, while the Germans had 47,000 troops and 250 tanks. The following day the Soviets captured Kingisepp, and the 59th Army drove into the right flank of the retreating 18th Army. The fate of the Cherkassy Pocket hinged on a relief attempt by the XXXXVII. Panzer Corps but they were stuck in thick mud due to a thaw. A few days later German units were under threat at Krivoi Rog and Nikopol as the Soviet 13th and 60th Armies captured Rovno and Lutsk. *Generaloberst* Karl-Adolf Hollidt, commander of the 6th Army, asked for permission to withdraw his command (he would be replaced a few months later). On 6 February the III. Panzer Corps' relief attempt was abandoned due to mud, a lack of fuel and enemy resistance, and the same factors were also hindering the XXXXVII. Panzer Corps. On 12 February, as the III. Panzer Corps approached the Cherkassy Pocket, there were fierce armoured clashes with the Soviets. The following day the Soviet forces completed the capture of Luga, Polna and Lyady. The Volkhov Front had lost 12,000 soldiers with 38,000 wounded, and the fight to rid German forces from the Soviet Union and the Eastern Front continued.

Knight's Cross Recipients

Recipients in order of being awarded.

NB: Underlined Christian names are those the subject chose to be known by.

Gottfried <u>Friedrich</u> Theodor GOLLWITZER
General der Infanterie

* 27 April 1889, Bullenheim-Kitzingen, Bavaria
+ 25 March 1977, Amberg, Bavaria

Knight's Cross: Awarded on 8 February 1943 as *Generalleutnant* and Commander of the 88th Infantry Division as part of the 2nd Army for actions on the southern sector of the Russian Front, particularly near Voronezh and Sumy. From March until June 1943 he was in the Reserves and was then given the temporary leadership of the LIII. Army Corps, where he saw action near Bryansk and Orel while attached to Army Group Centre. On 20 January 1944 Gollwitzer was promoted to *General der Infanterie* and he was appointed Commanding General of the LIII. Army Corps. In June his command, together

Friedrich Gollwitzer entered military service in August 1908 with Bavarian Infantry Regiment 13 and at the start of the First World War he served as a *Leutnant* and adjutant. He served mainly as a staff officer in the war and was promoted to *Hauptmann* in August 1918, remaining in the Army after the war. From October 1935 he served as Commander of Infantry Regiment 41 and was promoted to *Oberst* in January 1936 before seeing action in the Second World War as Commander of Division 193. Promoted to *Generalmajor* in October 1939, he was commander of the 88th Infantry Division from February 1940 and saw action in France from May. From June 1941 he took part in the invasion of the Soviet Union.

with the Staff of Army Group Centre, was destroyed and Gollwitzer was taken prisoner by the Soviets near Vitebsk. He remained in Soviet captivity until his release on 6 October 1955, when he was allowed to return to Germany.

Otto Fritz Hermann HEIDKÄMPER
Generalleutnant

* 13 March 1901, Lauenhagen, Schaumburg-Lippe
+ 16 February 1969, Bückeburg, Lower Saxony

Knight's Cross: Awarded on 8 February 1943 as *Oberst im Generalstab* and Chief of the General Staff of the XXIV. Panzer Corps part of Army Group B after taking full command of the Panzer Corps after the death of its commander, *Generalleutnant* Karl Eibl. He took over command of the corps with great success, and commanding 9,000 German soldiers and 11,000 Italians he led the panzer corps with great distinction for fourteen days while being cut off from other German units as well as his headquarters. It was his confidence, energy and leadership alone that saved almost 20,000 soldiers from capture or death and it was reported by other officers that *Oberst* Heidkämper repeatedly distinguished himself through personal bravery. From 5 May 1943 he was Chief of the General Staff of the 3rd Panzer Army under *Generaloberst* Hans-Georg Reinhardt on the Eastern Front, then from September, with the rank of *Generalmajor*, he served in a similar captivity with Army Group Centre under the same commander. Promoted to *Generalleutnant* on 9 November 1944, he took command of the 464th Infantry Replacement Division on 27 April 1945, seeing action on the Eastern Front while defending Saxony as part of the 4th Panzer Army. During the last weeks of the war his command fought with

Otto Heidkämper entered the Army as an officer candidate in July 1918 and briefly saw action before the war ended four months later. He remained in the Army after the war and was commissioned as a *Leutnant* in April 1922. Promoted to *Major* in August 1938, he served as Chief of Operations of the 2nd Light Division from May 1939 before being promoted to *Oberstleutnant* in November 1940. In June 1942 he was promoted to *Oberst* and went on to serve as Chief of the General Staff of the XXIV. Panzer Corps in the Soviet Union.

the 545th *Volksgrenadier* Division against the Americans and those that had not been killed, including Heidkämper, were taken prisoner on 9 May 1945.

<u>Fridolin</u> Rudolf Theodor von SENGER UND ETTERLIN
General der Panzertruppe

* 4 September 1891, Waldshut, Baden
+ 4 January 1963, Freiburg im Breisen, Baden-Württemberg

Knight's Cross: Awarded on 8 February 1943 as *Generalmajor* and Commander of the 17th Panzer Division while attached to the LVII. Panzer Corps for his distinguished leadership during the decisive battles between the Volga and the Don during the attempted relief of the 6th Army. It was also awarded for his part in the fighting along the Manych River in southern Russia, when his men pushed Soviet troops back across the river on 24 January 1943. Senger und Etterlin was promoted to *Generalleutnant* on 1 May and from 18 June served as German Liaison Officer to the Italian 6th Army, and at the same time he

Fridolin von Senger und Etterlin joined the Army in October 1910 but continued with his studies at Oxford, England, where he graduated with a diploma in political economy in 1914. He returned to Germany soon afterwards and saw action at the beginning of the war with the rank of *Leutnant*. He ended the war as an ordnance officer and stayed in the Army after the war, rising to the rank of *Major* in February 1934.

Senger und Etterlin held the rank of *Oberst* at the beginning of the Second World War and was serving as commander of the 3rd Cavalry Regiment in Göttingen. Later he served with the 1st Cavalry Division as a regimental commander with the rank of *Oberst*. From July 1940 he was chief of the German delegation to the Italian–French Armistice Commission and was promoted to *Generalmajor* in September 1941.

was Commander of German Armed Forces in Sicily. From September he was German commander in Sardinia and Corsica and from October 1943 he took over the leadership of the XIV. Panzer Corps in Italy.

Knight's Cross with Oakleaves: He became the 439th recipient on 5 April 1944 as *General der Panzertruppe* and Commanding General of the XIV. Panzer Corps as part of the 10th Army for his outstanding leadership of German forces at Monte Cassino. He was promoted to *General der Panzertruppe* in January and his abilities as a commander stood out during the first battle from 17 January until 18 February 1944. He was also outstanding during the fighting between 15 and 23 March 1944, which resulted in a complete German victory. Over the next few months the Allies suffered terrible casualties trying to recapture the town of Cassino and scale the heights dominated by the ruins of the Benedictine monastery. Senger und Etterlin was personally decorated with the Oakleaves by Hitler on 27 April 1944 at Hitler's official residence, the Berghof. In May the Allies finally broke through the Monte Cassino front and captured Rome in June, and after withdrawing to the Gothic Line, Senger's corps found itself defending Bologna. From October Senger und Etterlin was given the leadership of the 14th Army in Italy and in early May 1945 he was head negotiator of the German surrender in Italy. When this was over he went into British captivity until his release on 16 May 1948.

Georg SCHOLZE
Generalmajor

* 21 August 1897, Löbau, Saxony
+ 24 April 1945, Berlin-Wannsee, Berlin

Knight's Cross: Awarded on 17 February 1943 as *Oberst* and Commander of Motorised *Lehr* Regiment 901 of the 19th Panzer Division for his leadership during the defence of the village of Strelzowk in Belarus from early January 1943. He later saw action at the Kharkov counteroffensive of March 1943 and at the Kursk offensive in July of that year, where his unit suffered heavy casualties. Scholze later saw action near Zhitomir from November 1943 and during the withdrawal through northern Ukraine in March 1944. From July he was attached to the German Military Mission in Romania as an instructor for their armoured units, and for a few months he was attached to a combat Group with the 8th Army. From late November he attended the 16th Divisional Leaders Course in Hirschberg and in December attended a short course for panzer officers. On

Georg Scholze entered the Army as a war volunteer in August 1914 with Jäger Battalion 5 and was promoted to *Leutnant* in May 1915. He served as a platoon leader, battalion adjutant and company leader. He left the Army in 1919 and re-joined in 1934 as a *Hauptmann*, serving as a company commander with Infantry Regiment 9 in Potsdam. He was adjutant to the commander of the III. Army Corps at the beginning of the Second World War and was promoted to *Oberstleutnant* in June 1940 while commander of a battalion with Infantry Training Regiment in Döberitz.

10 February 1945 he took over the leadership of the 20th Panzer Grenadier Division in Silesia and from 16 April he took part in the Third Reich's last stand while defending the Seelow Heights just over 50 miles from Berlin. On 20 April he was promoted to *Generalmajor* and moved towards Berlin-Wannsee, where his command was crushed by Soviet forces and where on 24 April 1945 it was reported that Scholze committed suicide – his body has never been found.

<u>Gerd</u> Paul Valerian Georg Heinrich von BELOW
Generalmajor der Reserve

* 30 November 1892, Strasbourg, Uckemark
+ 8 December 1953, Prison Camp No. 48 in Vojkovo, Soviet Union

Knight's Cross: Awarded on 28 February 1943 as *Oberst der Reserve* and Commander of Grenadier Regiment 374 of the 227th Infantry Division for action during the Soviet campaign. On 19 January 1943 the remnants of Grenadier Regiment 347 were fighting Soviet troops near the Sinyavino Heights, east of Leningrad. Here his regiment launched a counter-attack against Soviet troops and retook a small village that had been captured by Russian forces. They had also closed the front-line gap that had secured the German grip on the Sinyavino Heights. Below was promoted to *Oberst der Reserve* in May. In October 1944 he was assigned to the 15th Divisional Leaders Course and from January 1945 he was delegated with the leadership of Special Purpose Division Staff 611. From February he took over as leader of Special Purpose Division Staff 615 and saw action on the Eastern Front. On 20 April he was promoted to *Generalmajor der Reserve* and his troops were resting in Dresden when they surrendered to Soviet troops on 8 May 1945.

Richard MÜLLER
Generalleutnant

* 4 November 1891, Emseloh, Saxony
+ 16 July 1943, north-east Orel, Soviet Union

Knight's Cross: Awarded on 7 March 1943 as *Generalleutnant* and Commander of the 211th Infantry Division as part of the 2nd Panzer Army for his outstanding service during the successful defence against enemy forces north of Orel. Between the end of February and early March 1943, against far superior Soviet forces, he personally rushed forward and hastily assembled his forces. He then led the main counter-attack under the heaviest of enemy fire and managed to stop a strong force of Soviet soldiers. Müller later took part in the opening phase of the Battle of Kursk and was killed north-east of Orel on 16 July 1943.

Richard Müller was attached to the Engineers in Schleswig-Holstein upon joining the Army in March 1911 with the rank of *Leutnant*. He served during the First World War as a platoon leader and a company leader and remained in the *Reichswehr* after the war serving with the Reich Defence Ministry. From October 1936 until August 1939 he served with three different engineer battalions in Rathenow and Wittenberg. He was promoted to *Oberst* in August 1938 and later served as Engineer Leader of Panzer Group Guderian on the Eastern Front.

Ernst Johann RUPP
Generalleutnant

* 13 January 1892, Landshut, Germany
+ 30 May 1943, Krymsk, Soviet Union

Knight's Cross: Awarded on 7 March 1943 as *Generalleutnant* and Commander of the 97th *Jäger* Division of the XXXXIV. Army Corps for actions during the Soviet winter offensive. He saw action during the campaign in the Caucasus region and in the subsequent retreats from the area. He was killed on 30 May 1943 near Krymsk on the northern slope of the Caucasus Mountains, and he is buried today in the German War Cemetery, Block 10, Row 48, Grave No. 3961 in Sebastopol, Ukraine.

Ernst Rupp joined the Army in June 1911 and was attached to the 2nd Lower Alsatian Infantry Regiment No. 137, being commissioned as a *Leutnant* two years later. In July 1917 he served as a regimental adjutant of Reserve Regiment 60 and in September the following year he was shot in the arm but soon recovered and remained in the Army after the war. In April 1933 he was promoted to *Major* and from October 1934 he was Chief of Operations of the 7th Division in Munich. At the beginning of the Second World War in September 1939 Rupp was Chief of Staff of the Border Guard section Command 2 and from October 1940, now with the rank of *Oberst*, he was commander of the 36th Infantry Regiment on occupation duties in France.

Karl Freiherr von LERSNER
Generalmajor

* 1 July 1898, Frankfurt am Main
+ 25 January 1943 near Orel, Soviet Union

Knight's Cross: Awarded posthumously on 12 March 1943 as *Oberst* and Commander of Grenadier Regiment 537 of the 385th Infantry Division for actions during the Battles of Kharkov on the Russian front. He later saw action near Stalingrad and managed to escape the Soviet encirclement, however his regiment was caught in the heavy fighting near Orel in January 1943, where Lersner was killed. He was posthumously awarded the Knight's Cross and promoted to the rank of *Generalmajor* on 20 April 1943. He has no grave.

Karl von Lersner entered the Army in May 1916 as an officer candidate, being commissioned as a *Leutnant* a year later. He stayed in the Army after the war, serving with Infantry Regiment 21, and from 1920 he served with Infantry Regiment 15. From October 1935 he served as company commander with Infantry Regiment 57 with the rank of *Hauptmann*. In February 1940 he was an *Oberstleutnant* and was battalion commander with Infantry Regiment 73. He was wounded in battle in May 1940 in France.

Heinz KOKOTT
Generalmajor

* 14 November 1900, Gross Strehlitz, Silesia
+ 29 May 1976, Siegsdorf, Bavaria

Knight's Cross: Awarded on 17 March 1943 as *Oberst* and Commander of Grenadier Regiment 337, part of the 208th Infantry Division, for actions on the Russian Front. He saw action near Orel as part of the 9th Army and fought with bravery and excellent leadership until he was wounded and admitted to hospital in June 1943. From September he was named as the Commander of School VI for Officer Candidates and from the end of June 1944 he served with Grenadier Brigade 1135 before being appointed leader of the 26th *Volksgrenadier* Division in September. The division had been almost destroyed during the Soviet summer offensive and was now being re-formed in western Poland, which included Army, *Luftwaffe* and Naval personnel. It was sent to Luxembourg on the Western Front in November and saw heavy fighting during the Battle of the Bulge, where Kokott was promoted to *Generalmajor* and his command was confirmed. His command of the XXXXVII. Panzer Corps performed well during the campaign, although it would suffer heavy casualties during the Siege of Bastogne. At the end of the offensive his command had a combat strength of 1,782 men, but remained in combat against the Allied drive on Prüm, Germany, from February 1945. Kokott ended the war in the Harz Mountain region in

Heinz Kokott entered Army service in October 1918 with Infantry Regiment 157 and remained in the Army after the war. He was commissioned as a *Leutnant* in February 1923 while attached to Infantry Regiment 7 and from June 1934 until October 1939 *Hauptmann* Kokott was an instructor at the Infantry School. Later he was appointed battalion commander with Infantry Regiment 196. He saw action in Poland and from June 1940 saw action in France. Promoted to *Oberstleutnant* in October 1941, he served as commander of the 178th Infantry Regiment from December, seeing action in the Soviet Union.

northern Germany, where he surrendered to US forces on 22 April 1945 and remained in Allied captivity until June 1947.

August <u>Karl-Wilhelm</u> von SCHLIEBEN
Generalleutnant

* 30 October 1894, Eisenach, Rhine Province
+ 18 June 1964, Giessen, Hesse, Germany

Knight's Cross: Awarded on 17 March 1943 as *Oberst* and Commander of Special Brigade 4 and Leader of the 208th Infantry Division as part of the 2nd Panzer Army for actions against Soviet troops around Shisdra near Orel. He was promoted to *Generalmajor* in May 1943 while commander of the 18th Panzer Division and took part in the Battle of Kursk, where his division was virtually destroyed. In the autumn of 1943 he led his division in the area around Kiev but in the autumn suffered heavy losses in the counteroffensive west of Kiev and his command was then disbanded. From December he took command of the 709th Infantry Division and was sent to Cherbourg in France, where Schlieben was also appointed Commandant of Cherbourg. In May 1944 he was promoted to *Generalleutnant* and on 23 June his command was redesignated 'Fortress' Cherbourg. Just three days later, with over 800 troops, he surrendered to Major General Manton S. Eddy, the commander of the US 9th Infantry Division, at Cherbourg. He was held at the prison camp for officers at Trent Park, north London, and was then transferred to Island Farm Special Camp 11, South Wales, in January 1946, where he remained until his release in October 1947.

Karl-Wilhelm von Schlieben is seen here shortly after surrendering to US forces in Cherbourg on 26 June 1944. He entered the Army in August 1914 and was assigned to the 3rd Guards Regiment, being commissioned as a *Leutnant* in March 1915. He served as a battalion adjutant and an ordnance officer, and remained in the Army after the war, serving with Mounted Regiment 12. From August 1934 he served with the 2nd Cavalry Brigade in Stettin and was promoted to *Major* in October 1935. He was appointed commander of Rifle Regiment 108 in August 1940.

Rolf SCHERENBERG
Generalmajor

* 27 May 1897, Berlin-Brandenburg
+ 10 September 1960, Villach, Carinthia, in Austria

Knight's Cross: Awarded on 26 March 1943 as *Oberst* and Commander of Grenadier Regiment 532 as part of the 383rd Infantry Division for his command while holding on to a wide sector south-east of Orel for a period of three days against very heavy attacks. Scherenberg saw action at Voronezh and in the early stages of the Stalingrad advance, and fought in the massive attacks on the 2nd Panzer Army by Soviet forces. He attended the 16th Divisional Leaders Course in Hirschberg from November until the end of December 1944, and took over, briefly the leadership of the 320th *Volksgrenadier* Division in February 1945. On 2 March he took over as leader of the 371st Infantry Division, seeing action in the Soviet Union and where on 20 April he was promoted to *Generalmajor* and his command of his division became official. He saw heavy fighting at Zhitomir in Ukraine, then in the Hube Pocket and later in southern Poland and in Silesia. He ended the war in the Deutsch-Brod Pocket east of Prague, where he was taken prisoner by the Soviets.

Friedrich-Carl von STEINKELLER
Generalmajor

* 28 March 1896, Deutsch Krone, Pomerania
+ 19 October 1981, Hannover, Lower Saxony

Knight's Cross: Awarded on 31 March 1943 as *Oberstleutnant* and Commander of Panzer Grenadier Regiment 7, part of the 7th Panzer Division, for his leadership during the defence of Slavyansk in Ukraine for several days against strong enemy pressure. He had also taken part in the Third Battle of Kharkov from March 1943 and saw action at Kursk, when the 7th Panzer Division was repulsed, and later during the battles around Kiev and Zhitomir. He was promoted to *Oberst* on 1 April 1943 and took over as deputy of the 7th Panzer Division while its commander Hasso von Manteuffel was on leave and from January 1944 he was on leave as part of the Führer Reserve. From February 1944 he attended the 9th Divisional Leaders Course in Hirschberg and in March he attended a course for Panzer officers. From April until 31 May he was delegated with the leadership of the Panzer Grenadier Division *Feldherrnhalle*

Friedrich-Carl von Steinkeller entered Ulanen Regiment 3 in August 1914 as a war volunteer and was commissioned as a *Leutnant* in May 1915. When the war was over he left the Army but rejoined in July 1934 as a company commander with the rank of *Hauptmann*. From October 1939 he was commander of the VI. Motorcycle Battalion, seeing action in Poland. He was wounded in July 1941 when his jeep ran over a mine and he spent the next five months recovering.

and from June 1944, after his promotion to the rank of *Generalmajor*, he took over as divisional commander. On the evening of 25 June about 100 Soviet tanks broke through the German lines near the Dnieper River and although Steinkeller managed to escape across the river he was wounded and captured near Berezina. He spent time in various Soviet prison camps, which included No. 62 in Kiev and Nr. 462 near Stalingrad, and he was sentenced to twenty-five years imprisonment and hard labour by a Soviet court in November 1948. He was eventually released on 8 October 1955.

<u>Ernst</u> Gottfried Karl Georg HACCIUS
Generalleutnant

* 11 December 1893, Hannover
\+ 11 February 1943, Vassiliev, Soviet Union

Knight's Cross: Awarded posthumously on 2 April 1943 as *Generalleutnant* and Commander of the 46th Infantry Division while attached to the XXXXIX. Army Corps

Ernst Haccius entered Army service in February 1914, and with his training complete he was assigned to Reserve Jäger Battalion 10. Commissioned as a *Leutnant* in December that year, he remained in the Army after the war before being appointed commander of the III. Battalion of Infantry Regiment 17 in October 1935 with the rank of *Major*. Promoted to *Oberstleutnant* in April 1937, he was appointed adjutant with the General Command of the X. Army Corps.

in recognition of his leadership during the Caucasus campaign and the latter stages of the Siege of Sevastopol. He was killed during an air attack near Vassiliev, Krasnodar, as Soviet commanders attempted to exploit the recent defeat of the German 6th Army at Stalingrad. Haccius was posthumously promoted to the rank of *Generalleutnant* and was replaced by *Oberst* Karl Le Suire.

Walther SCHELLER
Generalleutnant

* 27 January 1892, Hannover
+ 21 July 1944 near Brest-Litovsk, General Government [Poland]

Knight's Cross: Awarded on 3 April 1943 as *Generalleutnant* and Commander of the 9th Panzer Division as part of the 2nd Panzer Army for his success in the

defeat of a group of Soviet forces near Orel and in doing so he successfully prevented a hostile breakthrough attempt. Scheller took part in the opening weeks of the Battle of Kursk from July 1943 and from 20 October he was briefly given

Walther Scheller entered the Army as an officer candidate in February 1911, seeing action in the First World War with Infantry Regiment 82 and rising to the rank of *Oberleutnant* in January 1916. He was appointed orderly officer and then ordnance officer in December 1917, and remained in the Army after the war. He was appointed a General Staff Officer and from 1934 he was assigned to the Reich Ministry of Defence in Berlin.

Walther Scheller is seen here with the commander of Panzer Grenadier Regiment 11, *Oberstleutnant* Joachim Gutmann, who he has just presented with the Knight's Cross. Scheller became commander of the 8th Rifle Brigade in May 1941 and a month later took part in the invasion of the Soviet Union. In October he was promoted to *Generalmajor* and appointed commander of the 11th Panzer Division.

the leadership of the 334th Infantry Division. On 27 November he took over command of the 337th Infantry Division and saw action during the withdrawal at Rzhev, then at Yelnj, Smolensk and Orscha. From early March 1944 he served as Senior Field Commander 399 and served in the Soviet Union as part of the 2nd Army, deployed to the area of Brest-Litovsk. In June Scheller took over as Commandant of the area, where on 22 July 1944 he was killed in action when the Soviets stormed his headquarters. He has no known grave.

Fritz BECKER
Generalleutnant

* 7 March 1892, Heidberg, Hannover
+ 11 June 1967, Herzburg, Lower Saxony

Knight's Cross: Awarded on 6 April 1943 as *Generalmajor* and Commander of the 370th Infantry Division, part of the 17th Army, for his distinguished leadership during the fighting for the Kuban bridgehead, where his division successfully fended off all attacks made along the Protoka River in Ukraine by the Soviet 37th Army. He saw action on the Mius, at Rostov, in the Caucasus campaign and to the area near the Kuban Bridgehead, before being sent to the Lower Dnieper in the autumn of 1943. There his division suffered heavy losses. Becker, now with the rank of *Generalleutnant*, was sent on a divisional commander's course in June 1944. In July he briefly led the XXXXVI. Panzer Corps and from August he briefly took over command of the XXIV. Panzer Corps. On 30 September he was appointed Commander of the 389th Infantry Division and saw action

Fritz Becker entered the Army as a *Fahnenjunker* in January 1913 with Infantry Regiment 69, and in August 1914, at the start of the First World War, he was serving as a *Leutnant* and platoon leader with the I. Battalion. In September that same year he was wounded and hospitalised and in December he was transferred to Reserve Infantry Regiment 257. In July 1915, once fully recovered, he was appointed adjutant of the I. Battalion. By June the following year he had been promoted to *Oberleutnant* and was company leader, still with the same regiment. He stayed in the Army after the war, serving with different regiments before being assigned to Infantry Regiment 60 in August 1939, now with the rank of *Oberst.* He took part in the invasion of France in 1940.

in the Courland Pocket, returning to Germany in February 1945. He now took part in the defence of East Prussia and on 29 March, Becker was wounded and taken to hospital. He was released from hospital on 5 April and took command of Defence District Bremen until 26 April, when he was captured by British forces. He was held prisoner until 6 January 1948, when he returned to Germany.

Fritz MEYER
Generalmajor

* 23 December 1893, Hechthausen, Hannover
+ 17 February 1954, Wiesbaden, Hesse

Knight's Cross: Awarded on 6 April 1943 as *Generalmajor* and Commander of Supervisor of Construction Staff 7 for actions near Voronezh on the Russian Front. He commanded a battle group that was primarily composed of construction troops and managed to break out of the enemy's encirclement, forming a defensive stronghold. He served with the 2nd Army until mid-July 1943, and was attached to the Reserves until February 1944, when he served on the command staff of *Generalfeldmarschall* Gerd von Rundstedt the Commander-in-Chief West. From 15 February Meyer served as Commandant of Fortress Le Verdon in south-western France, where he served until 28 September 1944 when he was taken ill. He remained on sick leave until the end of the war and went into Allied captivity on 8 May 1945, being released in 1947.

Fritz Meyer entered the Army in March 1913, seeing action at the start of the First World War with Infantry Regiment 155 as a *Leutnant*. He remained in the Army after the war, rising to the rank of *Major* in July 1934 and taking over command of Engineer Battalion 46 from October 1935. From August 1939 he served on the staff of Pioneer Leader of the 1st Army and was promoted to *Oberst* in October that year.

Karl Freiherr von THÜNGEN-ROSSBACH
Generalleutnant

* 26 March 1893, Mainz, Hesse
+ 24 October 1944, Zuchthaus, Brandenburg-Görden

Knight's Cross: Awarded on 6 April 1943 as *Generalleutnant* and Commander of the 18th Panzer Division part of the XXXXI. Panzer Corps for actions on the southern sector of the Eastern Front, where Thüngen-Rossbach took part in the initial advances on Stalingrad. In June 1943 he was transferred and appointed Inspector General of Military Replacements in Berlin, where he made contact with officers involved in the plot to overthrow Hitler. At the time of the July 1944 bomb plot to kill Hitler, Thüngen-Rossbach was placed in command of Military District III, which was Berlin, but failed to act when he should have done and frittered away important time and opportunities. He was not sure if Hitler had been killed and was slow to react. He only arrived at Military District Command in Berlin to take charge at 7pm and at this point the attempted coup had failed. As a result he was arrested by the Gestapo on 7 August 1944 and discharged from the army. Now as a civilian he could be sentenced for his part in the plot by the People's Court in Berlin, where he was found guilty with the loss of all military honours and sentenced to death on 5 October 1944. On the orders of the Reich Minister of Justice Otto Thierack, he was executed by firing squad in the courtyard of the Brandenburg Prison on 24 October 1944.

Karl Freiherr von Thüngen entered Dragoon Regiment No. 5 in March 1912 and saw action during the First World War two years later as a *Leutnant*. He served as adjutant of the III. Battalion of the Royal Bavarian Infantry Regiment 24 from May 1915 and was promoted to *Oberleutnant* two years later. He remained in the Army after the war and from November 1933 he was serving in the Army Organisation Department, being promoted to *Major* a year later. In August 1939 he was appointed commander of Infantry Replacement Regiment 254 and from February 1940 he was commander of Mounted Regiment 22. From May took part in the invasion of France, now with the rank of *Oberst*.

Oskar ECKHOLT
Generalmajor

* 4 November 1894, Freisenbruch, Westphalia
+ 12 August 1982, Theesen, North-Rhine Westphalia

Knight's Cross: Awarded on 9 April 1943 as *Oberst* and Commander of Artillery Regiment 178, part of the 78th Sturm Division, for actions in Orel on the Russian Front with Army Group Centre. He stayed in Russia until the end of October 1943, and after some leave he attended the 8th Divisional Leaders Course from November. The following month he was attached to Army Group Centre and was later attached to the Staff of the 291st Infantry Division. On 15 January 1944 he took over as Leader of the 291st Infantry Division, which suffered heavy losses in northern Ukraine and later saw heavy action in the Kamenetz-Podelsk, known as the 'Hube Pocket'. On 1 April Eckholt was promoted to *Generalmajor* but during the Soviet offensive of 13 July, he was severely wounded and taken to a number of different military hospitals. He was so badly wounded that he never returned to action and while recovering in Heiligenstadt Hospital in Vienna, it was taken over by the Americans and Eckholt remained in US captivity until 23 May 1947.

Oskar Eckholt entered Army service with Foot Artillery Regiment 18 in March 1914 and was commissioned as a *Leutnant* in February 1915. From July 1916 he served as Photographic Officer while attached to the Staff of 14th Landwehr Division and was awarded both classes of the Iron Cross. He left the Army after the war, re-joining in April 1934 with the rank of *Hauptmann*, and was attached to various artillery regiments in East Prussia as a battalion commander.

Hans-Kurt Hermann HÖCKER
Generalleutnant

* 1 August 1894, Stadthagen, Schaumburg-Lippe
+ 10 August 1961, Detmold, North Rhine-Westphalia

Knight's Cross: Awarded on 14 April 1943 as *Generalleutnant* and Commander of the 258th Infantry Division of the IX. Army Corps for actions on the Russian

Front. He was personally presented with the Knight's Cross by the Commanding General of the XXXXVI. Panzer Corps *General der Infanterie* Hans Zorn. He later took part in the defensive battles at Jucknov, Gshatsk and Orel and from July 1943 saw action during the beginning of Kursk offensive. From November he served as Commander of the 17th *Luftwaffe* Field Division, taking it over from *Luftwaffe* staff when it was put under army control while on duty on the French Atlantic coast. During the spring of 1944 his division was camped near the Seine River east of Le Havre as part of the 15th Army. From late September until October he was attached to the Reserves before being named as the commander of the 167th *Volksgrenadier* Division, which had been newly formed after being virtually wiped out in the Cherkassy encirclement in early 1944. It was formed in Hungary and took recruits from the remnants of the 17th *Luftwaffe* Field Division and trained them in Slovakia, before being sent to Belgium in January 1945. He commanded the division during the latter stages of the Ardennes Offensive and his command remained on the Western Front until it was virtually crushed by the US 3rd Army in the Eifel district. Höcker went into US captivity on 26 April 1945, and remained there until his release on 7 June 1947.

Hans-Kurt Höcker entered military service in February 1912 and at the beginning of the First World War he saw action as a platoon leader with the 11th Company of Infantry Regiment 55. Captured by the French in October 1917, he remained in the Army after the war and rose to the rank of *Major* in October 1933. From 1934 until 1936 he served as an instructor at the War School in Dresden and Munich before taking over command of Infantry Regiment 487 in August 1939. He was appointed commander of the 258th Infantry Division in April 1942 with the rank of *Generalmajor*.

Hans-Joachim KAHLER
Generalmajor

* 21 March 1908, Morhange in Mörchingen, France
+ 14 January 2000, Hamburg

Knight's Cross: Awarded on 14 April 1943 as *Major* and Commander of Motorcycle Troop Battalion 34 of the 4th Panzer Division for actions on the Russian Front. On 4 March 1943 Kahler chose to launch an attack, without consulting his divisional commander, and succeeded in capturing the town of Ternopol in Ukraine. This yielded a prize of two important strategic bridges as well as a key railway embankment. This action enabled the railway to be reopened along the Sevedyna–Buda line, which allowed necessary supplies and equipment to be easily delivered to German troops for other attacks. From 7 May Kahler was named as leader of the Panzer Grenadier Regiment 33 and saw action in the opening phase of the attack on Kursk. From late August 1943 he was commander of Panzer Grenadier Regiment 5 while attached to the 12th Panzer Division and was promoted to *Oberstleutnant* in September while fighting in the Battles of Bryansk and Gomel and in the defensive battles in middle Dnieper from the autumn.

Knight's Cross with Oakleaves: He became the 355th recipient on 17 December 1943 as *Oberstleutnant* and Commander of Panzer Grenadier Regiment 5 of the 12th Panzer Division for continued actions on the Eastern Front. On 20 September 1943 the Soviets broke a key section of the

Hans-Joachim Kahler entered military service in April 1927, was promoted to the rank of *Leutnant* five years later and took over as Regimental Adjutant of Mounted Regiment 14. Promoted to *Rittmeister* in February 1938, he was appointed Squadron Commander in Reconnaissance Battalion 156 and in September 1939, at the beginning of the Second World War, he saw action during the invasion of Poland. A year later he was appointed adjutant of the 12th Panzer Division under *Generalmajor* Josef Harpe and saw action on the Eastern Front from June 1941.

German front line and captured an important village. Khaler led a Battle Group in a counter-attack that succeeded in capturing the town taken by the Soviets. By this action the Soviets were unable to take the main road leading to Repki and Gomel. It was all the more important because had this major road not been taken the German divisions would have been forced into an almost impassable swampy terrain that would have slowed down their advance and could have resulted in the loss of equipment or maybe even lives. As a result, Kahler was awarded the Oakleaves, which were personally presented to him by Hitler in early 1944 at the Berghof on the Obersalzburg in Austria. On 1 March Kahler was promoted to *Oberst* and from July he took over the leadership of Panzer

Grenadier Brigade *Grossdeutschland* and took part in heavy defensive fighting in East Prussia. In November his command was transferred to the Western Front and he took part in the Ardennes Offensive, where on 20 December he was severely wounded and hospitalised. On 31 January 1945, while lying in a hospital, he learned that he had been promoted to the rank of *Generalmajor* but he never commanded a front-line unit again. On 8 May he surrendered to British troops and in February the following year he was released.

Hans-Walter HEYNE
Generalleutnant

* 10 January 1894, Hannover
+ 29 August 1967, Ronnenberg

Knight's Cross: Awarded on 16 April 1943 as *Oberst* and Commander of Artillery Regiment 182 of the 82nd Infantry Division for actions on the Russian Front. The award was personally presented by the Commander of XIII Army Corps *Generalleutnant* Friedrich Siebert in late April 1943. On 1 June Heyne was promoted to *Generalmajor* and confirmed as Commander of the 82nd Infantry Division, seeing action in Kursk and Voronezh and in the actions around Kiev before the encirclement at Cherkassy, during which time he had been promoted to *Generalleutnant*. His command managed to break out of the encirclement but with heavy losses in the Hube Pocket his command was downgraded to Divisional Group 82 and was assigned to the 254th Infantry Division. After some leave, Heyne was appointed commander of the 6th Infantry Division in June 1944 and saw action in the Soviet Union as part

Hans-Walter Heyne entered Army service in February 1913 and served as battery officer and later adjutant with Artillery Regiment 25. He later served with Reserve Field Artillery Regiment 56 and ended the war with the rank of *Oberleutnant*, remaining in the Army. From 1926 he served with Mounted Regiment 3 and later attended cavalry school in Hannover, and later in Potsdam. In February 1930 he suffered a severe head injury during a fall from a horse and was finally appointed an active officer again in December 1940 as a battalion commander with Artillery Regiment 217.

of the XXXV. Army Corps. On 30 June his unit was captured by Soviet forces at Bobruysk and Heyne, together with most of his staff, were held in Soviet captivity until October 1955.

Werner HÜHNER
Generalleutnant

* 13 August 1886, Helmerkamp, Hannover
+ 19 February 1966, Plön, Schleswig-Holstein

Knight's Cross: Awarded on 18 April 1943 as *Generalleutnant* and Commander of the 61st Infantry Division while attached to the XXVIII. Army Corps for his personal bravery and leadership in the Soviet Union. During the winter of 1942 and early 1943 his forces took part in the Second Battle of Lake Ladoga and rescued the 227th Infantry Division, which had been encircled by elements of the Soviet armies near Schlüsselburg. He had been taken ill from 21 March until early May 1943 and after recovering he was briefly appointed commander of the 416th Infantry Division, but became unwell again. On 1 July he transferred to the Staff of the Command Office of Fortifications near Königsberg in Prussia and within two weeks was appointed Commandant. From February 1945 he was attached to the Military District Command II in Stettin, which later became a fortress in which Hühner was named as Commandant. He surrendered to British troops on 8 May 1945 and was held in captivity until 14 April 1947.

Werner Hühner saw action during the First World War with Infantry Regiment 51 and was wounded and hospitalised only a few days into the conflict. He later served as regimental adjutant, company leader and battalion commander, ending the war with the rank of *Hauptmann*. He stayed in the Army after the war and was appointed adjutant of the 1st Division in February 1933. By 1935 he held the rank of *Oberstleutnant* as adjutant of the I. Army Corps. He later took command of Infantry regiment 25 and from August 1941 he took over the leadership of the 8th Panzer Division with the rank of *Generalmajor*.

Ernst Heinrich VOSS
Generalmajor

* 3 November 1899, Timmenrode, Germany
+ 11 October 1943, Nowo-Lipowo, Ukraine

Knight's Cross: Awarded on 18 April 1943 as *Oberstleutnant* and Commander of Grenadier Regiment 585 part of the 320th Infantry Division for his outstanding leadership during fierce fighting in the southern sector of the Eastern Front. Although his men had no prior experience of fighting in the East when they arrived at the front in January 1943, Voss was able to fight a delaying action with his regiment despite superior Soviet numbers. His command later went on to achieve excellent success in the counter-offensive to recapture Kharkov from the Soviets and in June 1943 he was promoted to the rank of *Oberst*. During the summer and autumn he once again proved himself a capable commander during the battles for Belgorod.

Knight's Cross with Oakleaves: He became the 314th recipient posthumously on 28 October 1943 as *Oberst* and Commander of Grenadier Regiment 585 while part of the 320th Infantry Division for his command during the defensive fighting during the Battle of the Dnieper River between 5 and 10 October 1943. He successfully defended a wide sector of

Ernst Voss joined the police after the First World War and from October 1935 served as company commander of the 24th Infantry Regiment with the rank of *Hauptmann*. At the start of the Second World War, still with the same regiment, he served as battalion commander and was seriously wounded in October 1941 and transferred into the Führer Reserve. In January 1942 he was appointed commander of Infantry Replacement Battalion 24 and was promoted to *Oberstleutnant*, seeing action on the Eastern Front.

front against a breakthrough made by four Soviet divisions despite the fact that his regiment had already been weakened by heavy fighting. Voss was able to conduct a very successful defensive battle before being mortally wounded on 11 October by an anti-tank gun shell – in fact it was his sixth wound on the Eastern Front – and he was posthumously promoted to the rank of *Generalmajor*.

Hans WAGNER
Generalleutnant

* 11 March 1896, Saarbrücken, Rhine Province
+ 14 May 1967, Ulm, Baden-Württemberg

Knight's Cross: Awarded on 18 April 1943 as *Oberst* and Commander of Artillery Regiment 5, part of the 5th *Jäger* Division, for his leadership skills during the defensive battles south of Lake Ilmen. When strong enemy forces broke through the sector next to his division, he formed a battle group of artillerymen and drivers from his artillery regiment and they were able to intercept and prevent any further advance made by enemy forces. At the same time he had been delegated with the leadership of the 225th Infantry Division in the absence of its commander, and from June he took over the leadership of the 411th Grenadier Regiment. He briefly took command of the 32nd Infantry Division from mid-August 1943 and saw action in the northern sector of the Eastern Front. From September he attended the 7th Divisional Leaders Course at Döberitz and in November he was given the leadership of the 269th Infantry Division and was on occupation duty in Norway. In February 1944 Wagner was promoted to *Generalmajor* and his divisional command was confirmed. From October he saw action in the Vosges Mountains in Eastern France and later in the Battle of the Colmar Bridgehead on the Western Front.

Hans Wagner was a war volunteer from August 1914 and served in various regiments during the Conflict, being commissioned as a *Leutnant* in December 1916. From May 1920 he served with the security police in Prussia, rising to the rank of *Polizei-Major* in January 1935. From October that year he served with the Army and was attached to the 25th Artillery Regiment. From November 1938 he served as commander of the II. Battalion of Artillery Regiment 114, part of the 46th Infantry Division, seeing action in Poland in 1939 and then in Belgium and France from June 1940.

He was promoted to *Generalleutnant* in December and in January his command was transferred to southern Poland and was at this time of battle group strength only. He later saw action in Silesia and was in the Dresden area when news came that Berlin had fallen. He and most of his men managed to escape the area and on 8 May 1945 he surrendered to the Western Allies rather than the Soviets.

Walter Karl Hugo STETTNER RITTER VON GRABENHOFEN
Generalleutnant

* 19 March 1895, Munich, Bavaria
\+ 18 October 1944, Avala Hill, south Belgrade, Serbia

Knight's Cross: Awarded on 23 April 1943 as *Oberst* and Commander of the 1st Mountain Division while part of the XXXXIX. Mountain Army Corps for the major contribution he and his command achieved in the destruction of the Soviet 58th Army on the northern front of the Kuban Bridgehead. His division fought with great skill during the six-day battle, through difficult terrain and against superior enemy forces located in the swamps on the south of the Sea of Azov. On 1 February 1943 Stettner was promoted to *Generalmajor* as a direct result of his outstanding leadership of his division. The result of the German victory included the capture of 1,000 Soviet prisoners as well as sixty-nine guns and more than 250 mortars and machine guns. Later his division was withdrawn from the front and sent to Serbia and northern Greece, where it took part in anti-partisan operations. The division was fighting south of Belgrade in October 1944 when Stettner was killed in action on Avala Hill south of Belgrade and posthumously promoted to *Generalleutnant*.

Walter Stettner Ritter von Grabenhofen served as a cadet from 1908 and then joined the 11th Company of the Bavarian Infantry Regiment at the beginning of the First World War. He was wounded in July 1916 and remained with the Army after the war, apart from almost three years' service with the *Freikorps* from February 1919. He later served with Infantry Regiment 19, rising to the rank of *Major* in 1935. Then from October 1937 for the next three years he was a battalion commander with Mountain Jäger Regiment 98, part of the 1st Mountain Division.

Otto Heinrich Andreas TIEMANN
General der Pioniere

* 12 February 1890, Vilsen Hannover
+ 20 April 1952, Bruchhausen, Lower Saxony

Knight's Cross: Awarded on 28 April 1943 as *Generalleutnant* and Commander of the 93rd Infantry Division while attached to the II. Army Corps for his part in the defence of the Cholm sector during the winter of 1942–43 under very difficult circumstances. In the spring of 1943 his command was rested and sent to Poland to rest and refit, and later was assigned to France. He then entered the Reserves and from January 1944 was assigned to a course for commanding generals. Shortly after he was given the leadership of the XXIII. Army Corps, which as part of the 2nd Army saw action on the Eastern Front. He was promoted to *General der Pioniere* in May 1944 and saw action north of Brest-Litvosk, fighting his way back to the northern Bug River area. In mid-December he was appointed commanding general of the XVII. Army Corps, seeing action in Hungary, and from February 1945 his command moved from the Carpathians while attached to the 17th Army in Silesia. In May his command was captured in the Gitschin area when it was encircled by Allied forces and he was taken prisoner, being released in 1947.

Otto Tiemann entered the Army in 1908, trained as an officer and served as a battalion adjutant at the start of the First World War with the rank of *Leutnant*. He later commanded a mortar company, became a battery leader and was promoted to *Hauptmann* in December 1916. He remained in the Army after the war, rising to the rank of *Generalmajor* in October 1937, when he was serving as commander of the 93rd Infantry Division.

Gustav Hans Erdmann <u>Hellmut</u> von der CHEVALLERIE
Generalleutnant

* 9 November 1896, Berlin

+ 1 June 1965, Wiesbaden, Hesse

Knight's Cross: Awarded on 30 April 1943 as *Generalmajor* and Commander of the 13th Panzer Division for his part in the smashing of the Soviet 56th Army between 14th and 17 April 1943. During the defensive fighting near Krymskaya, a Soviet breakthrough attempt by five divisions and two large tank formations were defeated. Promoted to *Generalleutnant* on 1 May 1943, two weeks later Chevallerie was named as commander of the 13th Panzer Division. He saw action in the Dnieper battles in Ukraine and near Kharkov, where he was wounded on 25 October and transferred to the Reserves to recover. On 15 November he was appointed commander of the newly created 273rd Reserve Panzer Division. It was sent to France shortly after it had been formed as part of the 1st Army, where it guarded a sector between Bordeaux and the Spanish frontier. From May Chevallerie entered the Reserves once again and from 15 August he took temporary leadership of the 233rd Reserve Panzer Division before being appointed Commandant of the Panzer Training Grounds in Bergen in November. From 1 April 1945 until the end of the war he was Commander West Sudetenland, where he surrendered to Allied troops on 9 May, being released from in June 1947.

Hellmut von der Chevallerie was a war volunteer in August 1914 and was wounded twice, ending the war as a British prisoner in October 1917. After the war he joined the *Freikorps* and then the *Reichswehr* with Infantry Regiment 4, being promoted to *Rittmeister* in February 1931. From 1935 he transferred to the staff of the Inspector of Cavalry and then served with the X. and XII. Army Corps, where he saw action at the beginning of the Second World War with the rank of *Oberstleutnant*. In June 1940 he was attached to the 10th Panzer Division, took command of the division from August 1942 and was promoted to *Generalmajor* two months later.

Georg HACHTEL
Generalmajor

* 29 June 1894, Reubach, Württemberg
+ 20 July 1943, Konstanz in Baden, Germany

Knight's Cross: Awarded on 30 April 1943 as *Oberst* and Commander of *Jäger* Regiment 56, part of the 5th *Jäger* Division, for actions during the battles around Staraya Russa in the Soviet Union. He took part in the fighting between 15 and 28 February, seeing action as part of the Demjansk Offensive during the Soviet offensive known as Operation Polar Star. It was a German success that held the Demjansk area for two months and by March the Soviets had caused the Germans to withdraw and eventually retreat, and as a result the German attack on Moscow was ended. During this time Hachtel became ill and on 23 April took some leave. While at home he heard he had been awarded the Knight's Cross. Shortly afterwards he was admitted to a military hospital for treatment and later allowed home, where on 20 July where he died. He was posthumously promoted to the rank of *Generalmajor*.

Georg Hachtel entered Army service as a *Leutnant* with Fusilier Regiment 122 in March 1913, serving as a platoon leader, battalion adjutant and company leader throughout the First World War. He entered the *Reichswehr* in October 1919 with the rank of *Oberleutnant* and retired from the Army four years later. He returned to Army service in July 1934 with Infantry Regiment 75 and with the rank of *Hauptmann* and was appointed commander of the III. Battalion of his regiment in August 1935. He was appointed adjutant with the General Command of the V. Army Corps from May 1940 and promoted to *Oberst* in February 1942.

Erich Hermann SCHOPPER
Generalleutnant

* 2 July 1892, Zeulenroda, Reuss
+ 18 August 1978, Minden, North Rhine-Westphalia

Knight's Cross: Awarded on 30 April 1943 as *Generalleutnant* and Commander of the 81st Infantry Division of the XXVIII. Army Corps for his leadership and success on the Russian Front. He successfully led his forces against eight rifle divisions, four rifle brigades and five tank regiments over a four-week period south of Lake Ilmen in the Soviet Union. He took part in the latter stages of the Siege of Leningrad at Nevel and also took part in the retreat from Leningrad. By September 1943 his command had lost so many men that it was down to just six grenadier battalions and its artillery regiment had only three batteries left. From early April 1944 until July he was attached to the reserves and was then appointed to Higher Artillery Commander 310 as part of the 8th Army, seeing action in Hungary and the Carpathians until October 1944. He ended the war in Upper Austria and surrendered to Allied troops on 8 May 1945. He remained a prisoner of war until he was released in mid-1947.

Erich Shopper served with the Royal Prussian Army from November 1912 and at the beginning of the First World War he was a battery officer with Field Artillery Regiment 74 with the rank of *Leutnant*. Promoted to *Oberleutnant* in October 1916, he later served as an adjutant of Artillery Commander 98 and remained in the Army after the war. In October 1935 he was commander of I. Batalion of Artillery Regiment 39 and was promoted to *Oberstleutnant* in 1936. He was appointed commander of Artillery Regiment 6 in April 1938 and by November 1940, now with the rank of *Oberst*, he had been appointed commander of Artillery Commander 137.

Erich SCHNEIDER
Generalleutnant

* 12 August 1894, Biedenkopf, Hesse
+ 3 October 1980, Wiesbaden, Hesse

Knight's Cross: Awarded on 5 May 1943 as *Generalmajor* and Commander of the 4th Panzer Division while attached to the 2nd Army for recognition for his outstanding leadership and for actions on the Russian Front. He led his forces during the encirclement and crushed strong Soviet forces that posed a threat to his open flanks and in doing so closed the gap in the front line south-west of Orel. From June he was head of the department for Weapons Testing in the Army Ordnance Office of the High Command. Schneider was promoted to *Generalleutnant* in July 1943 and from December 1944 he was named commander of the 14th Motorised Infantry Division.

Erich Schneider entered the Army in 1914 with Fusilier Regiment 13 and served as a battalion and regimental adjutant. He stayed in the Army after the war and by August 1937 he had been promoted to *Oberstleutnant* and was attached to Artillery Regiment 75 as a battalion commander. In January 1940 he was promoted to *Oberst* and later became commander of Artillery Regiment 103 while attached to the 4th Panzer Division, seeing action in France.

Knight's Cross with Oakleaves: He became the 768th recipient on 6 March 1945 as *Generalleutnant* and Commander of the 14th Motorised Infantry Division as part of the XXVI. Army Corps for his bravery and distinguished service during the fierce fighting in East Prussia. He took part in a five-day battle west of Ostrołęka, which saw repeated Soviet attacks pushed back and defeated. Schneider was found to be right at the front of his troops during the many attacks and was able to make his decisions based on a clear understanding of the situation as well as provide an inspiring example to his troops. He was wounded on 21 March 1945 and was relieved of his command, not just because of his wound but because he opposed orders that had come directly from Hitler and he spent a brief period of time in a Gestapo prison. No proof of any crime could be found and he surrendered to Allied troops in May 1945, remaining in Allied captivity until August 1947.

Otto BARTH
Generalmajor

* 18 June 1891, Dresden
+ 3 May 1963, Erlangen, Bavaria

Knight's Cross: Awarded on 8 May 1943 as *Oberst* and Commander of Artillery Regiment 117 while attached to the 111th Infantry Division in recognition of his leadership during the heavy fighting in the Kuban bridgehead area near the River Mius. He was attached to Artillery School 1 from September 1943, returning to front-line duty in August the following year as Commander of the 30th Infantry Division. By October his division was in retreat through the Courland via Riga and fought in various battles towards the end of the year. On 9 November Barth was promoted to *Generalmajor*, and from February 1945 he was appointed Commander of the 21st Air Landing Field Division, part of Army Corps XVI. Barth once again took part in fighting in the Courland area against Soviet forces, and was taken prisoner on 8 May 1945. He remained a Soviet prisoner until 9 October 1955, having been convicted and found guilty of being a war criminal by a Soviet military court.

Otto Barth saw action from May 1940 in the Battle of France, where he led his battalion through Luxembourg during the opening stages of the campaign and remained in France on occupation duty when the country surrendered. He was promoted to *Oberstleutnant* in August 1940, and from December served as Commander of Artillery Regiment 117. His regiment was transferred to the General Government in Poland in June 1941, and from there he took part in the invasion of the Soviet Union. His regiment crossed the Bug River and marched to the area east of Poltava. From 1942 he took part in the advance into the Caucasus and led his regiment through Shakhty, Rostov and Novorossiysk.

Wolf-Günther TRIERENBERG
Generalleutnant

* 18 June 1891, Forst-Lausitz, Brandenburg
+ 25 July 1981, Masebeck, North Rhine-Westphalia

Knight's Cross: Awarded on 10 May 1943 as *Generalleutnant* and Commander of the 167th Infantry Division, part of Army Group South, for actions near Kharkov in the Soviet Union. He saw action as part of the 2nd Panzer Army in the final thrusts toward Moscow in September 1941, and later was sent to

Wolf-Günther Trierenberg entered the Army in March 1910 and saw action in the First World War with Fusilier Regiment 38. Promoted to *Oberleutnant* in September 1915, he served as battalion adjutant and later on the staff of the 11th Infantry Division. He was promoted to *Hauptmann* in October 1918 and stayed with the Army after the war, serving as a staff officer with various divisions. By August 1937 he had been promoted to *Oberst* and from early 1939 he served as Chief of Staff of the Commander of the VI. Army Corps in Münster.

Generalleutnant Trierenberg, seen here in Russia as commander of the 167th Infantry Division, which he took command of in August 1941.

the Haarlem sector of Holland to rest and refit. His command remained on occupation duty until early 1943, when Trierenberg returned to the Eastern Front. In December 1943 he was appointed commander of the 347th Infantry Division and was sent to Holland, where he remained until the summer of 1944 when his division was sent into battle on the Western Front. He was sent to France and was caught up in the retreat from Normandy, where his division suffered heavy losses at Charleville, at Fort Ymuiden in Lille, France. He later took part in the retreats into Belgium, and in the Siegfried Line battles on the German frontier. From the end of March 1944 he was also for about one week deputy commanding general of the LXXXVIII. Army Corps. In September Trierenberg, together with the 347th Infantry Division, was back in action on the Siegfried Line, and fought at Schleiden in the Eifel mountain area and later from January 1945 saw action near Saarlautern. Trierenberg was wounded in early April and surrendered to US troops in Thüringen on 8 May 1945. Curiously, his division had been redesignated the 347th *Volksgrenadier* Division on 7 May – one day before the end of hostilities.

Otto-Ernst Fritz Adolf REMER
Generalmajor

* 18 August 1912, Neubrandenburg, Mecklenburg-Strelitz
+ 4 October 1997, Malaga, Andalucia in Spain

Knight's Cross: Awarded on 18 May 1943 as *Major* and Commander of the I. Battalion of Motorised Grenadier Regiment *Grossdeutschland* of Motorised Infantry Division [motorised] *GD* for his leadership during the intense fourteen days of combat during the Battle of Kharkov in early 1943. Remer's troops, mounted in halftracks and other armoured vehicles, covered the withdrawal of an entire Waffen-SS Panzer Corps during the

Major Otto-Ernst Remer wearing the Knight's Cross as Commander of the I. Battalion of Rifle Regiment 10, part of the 9th Panzer Division.

fierce fighting near Kharkov. From July his battalion saw heavy action as part of Operation Citadel at the Battle of Kursk, and once again in the defensive battles near Kharkov and during the Battle of Poltava.

Knight's Cross with Oakleaves: He became the 325th recipient on 12 November 1943 as *Major* and Commander of the I. Battalion of Motorised Grenadier Regiment '*GD*' of Panzer Grenadier Division '*GD*' for continued actions on the Russian front. Remer had proven himself as a talented battalion commander during the heavy fighting in the summer of 1943. During the thrust into the enemy area north of Belgorod Remer's battalion formed a small bridgehead and successfully defended against the various Soviet attacks. Towards the end of August

Remer wearing his Knight's Cross with Oakleaves as *Generalmajor* and Commander of the *Führer Begleit* Division.

1943 his battalion was employed in attacks against some high ground that had been occupied by Soviet forces west of Kharkov. The hill was captured, but then the Soviets appeared in the rear of the German grenadiers and during the strong enemy fire Remer led the attack from his armoured personnel carrier. However, due to his radio being knocked out he stood up in his vehicle and directed his troops despite the hail of bullets all around him. He was seriously wounded in March 1944 and although still listed as commander of his regiment he took time off to recover. In May he was appointed commander of Guard Regiment *Grossdeutschland* in Berlin and on 20 July, the day of the attempt on Hitler's life, he was ordered by the conspirators to arrest Goebbels at the War Ministry. Goebbels, however, managed to dissuade Remer from arresting him and got him to speak to Hitler on the phone. Hitler ordered Remer to arrest the conspirators, which he did. That same night he was promoted to *Oberst* by Hitler, skipping the rank of *Oberstleutnant*, and was personally thanked by the Führer for playing a major role in bring down the attempt to overthrow Hitler. In August he was appointed Commander of *Führer Begleit* Brigade at *Führer* Headquarters at Rastenburg. He later saw action during the Ardennes Offensive in December 1944. On 30 January 1945 Remer was promoted to *Generalmajor* and his command was expanded to divisional level. He was captured by US forces at the end of the war and after being released in 1947 he got into politics and formed a right-wing party that was later banned after attracting more than 360,000 supporters. In his later years he settled in Spain but still supported pro-Nazi groups and even questioned the Holocaust.

Robert MEISSNER
Generalleutnant

* 23 December 1888, Vienna, Austro-Hungary
+ 8 August 1953, Pervouralsk, Soviet Union

Knight's Cross: Awarded on 24 May 1943 as *Generalleutnant* and Commander of the 68th Infantry Division of the VII. Army Corps for actions on the southern sector of the Soviet Front. He was later assigned to the Army Supreme Court Martial Office and was for a time a judge at the Supreme Court in Torgau, dealing with courts martial. From mid-September 1944 Meissner entered the Reserves due to illness and from early October he was appointed commander of the Central Court of the Army in Berlin, where he served until the end of the war. He was taken prisoner by Soviet troops in Prague in May 1945 and sent to the Soviet Union, where he was tried and sentenced to twenty-five years hard labour by a military tribunal near Voronezh in May 1949. During his time in Soviet captivity he was transferred to at least seven different prison camps and he died from stomach cancer on 8 August 1953. He is buried at the cemetery of the Special Hospital 1893 in grave number twelve in Pervouralsk a city in Sverdlovsk, Soviet Union.

Robert Meissner joined the Austrian army in October 1904 as a cadet and served as a company leader in the opening stages of the First World War. In March 1917 he served as a General Staff Officer with the rank of *Hauptmann*, and when the war finished he remained in the Army. From March 1938 he served as a staff officer as part of the German Army after the Anschluss and was assigned to Army Group Command 5 in Vienna. At the beginning of the Second World War he was Chief of the Staff of the Deputy of the XII. Army Corps in Wiesbaden with the rank of *Oberst*.

Ferdinand NOELDECHEN
Generalleutnant

* 26 April 1895, Stargart, Prussia
+ 19 October 1951, Hamburg, Lower Saxony

Knight's Cross: Awarded on 8 June 1943 as *Generalmajor* and Commander of the 96th Infantry Division part of the XXVIII. Army Corps for actions during the tough defensive fighting south of Lake Ladoga in the Soviet Union. Noeldechen, as commander, inspired the grenadiers of his division to launch a counter-attack against the Soviets that had penetrated the German lines and so succeeded in both eliminating the enemy and restoring order to the German front. Shortly after being awarded the Knight's Cross, Noeldechen was promoted to the rank of *Generalleutnant* and continued to see action near Leningrad until late July 1943, when he entered the reserves for some leave. In November 1943 he returned to front-line duty as Commander of Division No. 438 and was made responsible for guarding the former German–Yugoslav frontier in the south-eastern part of the XVIII. Military District. It was later redesignated the 438th Special Purposes Divisional Command in late 1943 and Noeldechen continued to command it while it performed security duties until the end of the war.

Friedrich 'Fritz' von SCOTTI
Generalleutnant

* 3 May 1889, Offenbach am Main, Hesse
+ 16 July 1969, Karlsruhe, Baden-Württemberg

Knight's Cross: Awarded on 8 June 1943 as *Generalleutnant* and Commander of the 227th Infantry Division of the I. Army Corps for actions near Schlüsselburg on the southern shore of Lake Ladoga in the district of Leningrad in the Soviet Union. He later took command of the 80th Panzer Artillery Regiment while attached to the 8th Panzer Division, seeing action in northern Ukraine. Scotti was then appointed Higher Artillery Commander 304 while attached to the 17th Army, and from June 1944 he served in a similar capacity while attached to the 11th Army. He saw action in southern Ukraine until late January 1945, when he was relieved of his command and placed on the Reserve list. On 12 April he was taken prisoner by US troops and in June he was taken to a French prison camp near Calais, from which he later escaped. While trying to evade capture, Scotti

Friedrich von Scotti joined the Army in March 1907, seeing action during the First World War with Field Artillery Regiment 2. He remained with the Army after the war and from January 1933 served as an instructor at the Artillery School in Jüterbog with the rank of *Oberstleutnant*. From November 1938 he served with Artillery Commander 35 and in 1940 saw action during the invasion of France with the rank of *Generalmajor*.

was wounded and once recaptured he was taken to the former SS hospital in Germany and from there onto Neu-Ulm in Bavaria, where he remained until his release in late 1946.

Hermann von WEDEL
Generalmajor

* 27 July 1893, Magdeburg
+ 5 February 1944, Tartu, Estonia [Field hospital]

Knight's Cross: Awarded on 8 June 1943 as *Oberst* and Commander of Grenadier Regiment 590, part of the 321st Infantry Division, for his leadership during the defensive fighting north-west of Orel when a large amount of enemy forces managed to achieve a penetration of German lines. Wedel placed himself at the head of just twenty-five grenadiers from his regiment and they managed to eliminate this enemy penetration by mounting a successful counter-attack. Wedel had been sent to the Soviet Union in December 1942 and on 1 June 1943 he was promoted to *Generalmajor*. By September the following year his command had suffered heavy casualties at Bryansk and Rogachev and by October

Hermann von Wedel joined the Army in June 1911 and saw action during the First World War, being seriously wounded in September 1914. He returned to action, only to be taken prisoner by British forces in November 1917, and when the war was over he joined the police in January 1920, re-joining the Army in 1935 with the rank of *Major*. A year later he was made a battalion commander with Infantry Regiment 80, and from August 1939 he was commander of Infantry Regiment 208 and promoted to *Oberst* in December of that year.

the 321st Infantry Division to which his regiment was attached had practically ceased to exist. On 5 November he transferred as commander of the 10th *Luftwaffe* Field Division and saw action during the Siege of Leningrad from January 1944. On 29 January Wedel was seriously wounded during the Battle of Narva and was taken to a Military Field Hospital in Tartu, Estonia, where he died from his wounds on 5 January 1944.

Walther KRAUSE
Generalleutnant

* 31 December 1890, Schweidnitz, Silesia
+ 25 October 1960, Göttingen, Lower Saxony

Knight's Cross: Awarded on 10 June 1943 as *Generalmajor* and Commander of the 170th Infantry Division, part of the L. Army Corps, for actions during the Soviet winter offensive near Leningrad against heavy Soviet attacks. He was presented with the Knight's Cross by the Commander-in-Chief of the 18th Army, *Generaloberst* Georg Lindemann. In September Krause was promoted to *Generalleutnant* and later his division fought as part of Army Group North throughout 1943, and his division suffered heavy losses when the Soviets finally broke the siege at Leningrad in January 1944. In mid-July 1944 he took command of Division 462, which had been reorganised following D-Day in June, and he was sent into battle following the collapse of the German front

Walther Krause is seen here being decorated with the Knight's Cross by the Commander-in-Chief of the 18th Army *Generaloberst* Georg Lindemann. Krause entered the Army in 1909 and served during the First World War as platoon leader, an adjutant and later as a company leader, ending the war with the rank of *Oberleutnant*. He remained in the Army after the war and was appointed commander of Infantry Regiment 96 with the rank of *Oberst* at the start of the Second World War in 1939.

in Normandy. From 15 October Krause was commander of Rear Army Area 593 in Ukraine area as part of the staff of the 6th Army. He surrendered to US forces on 8 May 1945 and remained in captivity until his release in June 1947.

Erich KAHSNITZ
Generalmajor

* 17 February 1898, Insterburg
+ 29 July 1943, Breslau Hospital

Knight's Cross: Awarded on 15 July 1943 as *Oberst* and Commander of Füsilier Regiment *Grossdeutschland* while attached to Infantry Division *Grossdeutschland* for his outstanding leadership during the first day of the Battle of Kursk. During the breach of the heavily fortified Soviet field positions Kahsnitz's regiment lost their armoured support and the commander of the III. Battalion was killed by a mine, and the attack was called off. However, following his own assessment of the situation, Kahsnitz decided to renew the attack with his own regiment and despite tough opposing forces his command managed to break the Soviet defences and seize the enemy position, giving the Germans the higher ground. His commanders considered his accomplishments on a single day of fighting highly praiseworthy. However, on 3 July 1943 Kahsnitz was seriously wounded during one of the last counter-attacks near Belgorod and while in hospital in Breslau the award for the Knight's Cross came through after only ten days. The award was left next to his hospital bed for all to see, however on 29 July he succumbed to his wounds and died. He was posthumously promoted to *Generalmajor*.

Kurt MÖHRING
Generalleutnant

* 3 January 1900, Gross-Lipschin, Western Prussia
\+ 18 December 1944, near Beufort, Luxembourg

Knight's Cross: Awarded on 18 July 1943 as *Oberst* and Commander of Grenadier Regiment 82 of the 31st Infantry Division for actions during the Soviet winter offensive and for his bravery during the Battle of Kursk. Later he took part in the battles of the middle Dnieper and in the subsequent retreats through Russia. From 16 November until mid-December 1943 he attended the 8th Divisional Leaders Course in Döberitz-Elsgrund, and from December he took the leadership of the 196th Infantry Division and saw action in the Soviet Union as part of Army Group Centre. He was promoted to *Generalmajor* in March 1944 and his division command was confirmed. He continued to see heavy action in Russia until June, when he was transferred into the Reserves. On 25 September he took command of the 276th *Volksgrenadier* Division and saw action in Belgium and in the Ardennes, where on 18 December Möhring was killed during the first days of the Battle of the Bulge. He was posthumously promoted to the rank of *Generalleutnant* on 18 December 1944.

Johannes 'Hanns' FRIESSNER
Generaloberst

* 22 March 1892, Chemnitz, Saxony
\+ 26 June 1971, Gmain, Bavaria

Knight's Cross: Awarded on 23 July 1943 as *General der Infanterie* and Commanding General of the XXIII. Army Corps, part of the 2nd Panzer Army, for his actions during Operation Citadel, the German offensive against Soviet forces in the Kursk salient. On 5 and 6 July his forces captured the key village of Protassowo despite strong Soviet artillery fire and ten days later he achieved a major defensive success when his forces destroyed sixty-one Soviet tanks. Friessner remained Commanding General of the XXIII. Army Corps until the end of January 1944, and between 15 December 1943 and 7 January 1944 he was named as temporary commander of the 4th Army.

Knight's Cross with Oakleaves: He became the 445th recipient on 9 April 1944 as *General der Infanterie* and *Führer* of Army Detachment *Narva* while attached to Army Group North, for his outstanding leadership on the northern sector of the Soviet Front. He was presented with the Oakleaves personally by Hitler in September 1944 at *Führer* headquarters, the Wolf's Lair, in Rastenburg. In early July Friessner was appointed Commander-in-Chief of Army Group North and was promoted to *Generaloberst* on 23 July. Two days later he took command of Army Group South Ukraine, which became Army Group South from 23 September – during which time he was unable to halt the four-month Soviet offensive. On 23 December 1944 he was relieved of his command by Hitler and blamed for the failure of the offensive against the Soviet forces. He never took another command, remaining on the Reserves List until the end of the war. He surrendered to US forces on 8 May

Johannes 'Hanns' Friessner entered the Army in March 1911 and was commissioned as a *Leutnant* the following year. He served as adjutant of I. Battalion of Infantry Regiment 179 at the start of the First World War. He remained in the Army after the war and by 1933 had been promoted to *Major* and was serving as adjutant and tactics instructor at the Infantry School in Dresden. In March 1938 he was appointed Chief of Staff of the Inspector of War Schools in Berlin and from May 1942, with the rank of *Generalmajor*, he was made commander of the 102nd Infantry Division, part of the 9th Army during the invasion of the Soviet Union.

1945 and remained in American captivity until his release on 17 November 1947. In September 1951 Friessner was elected chairman of the Union of German Soldiers but resigned in December that year after it was reported he had justified the invasion of Poland as a legitimate measure to 'protect the ethnic Germans in Poland' at a press conference.

Arthur HAUFFE
General der Infanterie

* 20 December 1891, Wittgensdorf, Saxony
+ 22 July 1944, near Knyazhe, Ukraine

Knight's Cross: Awarded on 25 July 1943 as *Generalleutnant* and Commander of the 46th Infantry Division of the XXXX. Panzer Corps for actions during the heavy fighting near Zaporizhzhia, a city on the Dnieper River in south-eastern Ukraine. Hauffe was a veteran General Staff Officer with thirty years' service, was promoted to *General der Infanterie* and took over as Commanding General of the XIII. Army Corps on 1 November 1943. From June 1944 he saw action at Brody on the Russian Front, where his corps had been surrounded by Soviet troops and had to be rescued by a panzer division. There was a plan to attack once again in the same area in July and Hauffe was of the opinion that a second encirclement was to tempt fate, but it was clear the Russians were building up to attack the flanks of his Army Corps. On 13 July the Russians attacked with a tremendous artillery bombardment and his troops were met with Soviet T-34 tanks, supported by infantry, artillery and fighter-bomber aircraft. To the south, the Red Army broke through the lines of the XIII. Army and XXXXVIII. Panzer Corps. *Generaloberst* Josef Harpe, the commander of Army Group North Ukraine, had committed various army and panzer corps to the battle but by 15 July the 8th Panzer Division had been almost destroyed. Hauffe received no orders to withdraw and failed to act on his own initiative. He had spent much of the war in administrative posts, which included almost two and a half years as Chief of the German Military Mission in Romania. He was perhaps out of his depth and it was not until 18 July that he received orders to withdraw, but by then it was too late. Two days later it was reported that Hauffe had gone missing, having made his own way back to his headquarters. Two days later, while travelling he was captured, together with some of his staff, by Soviet forces near Knyazhe in Ukraine and while marching into captivity he stepped on a mine and was killed.

Martin Moritz BIEBER
Generalmajor

* 10 November 1900, Bad Tabarz, Thüringen
+ 19 October 1974, Düsseldorf

Knight's Cross: Awarded on 28 July 1943 as *Oberst* and Commander of Grenadier Regiment 184 while attached to the 86th Infantry Division for actions during Operation Citadel, the German offensive in the Kursk salient. On 5 July, the first day of the attack, his command managed to break through the enemy defensive positions. He had no contact with higher commands for just over an hour and at about 1600 he decided, on his own initiative, to launch an attack with five tanks and twenty-five mounted infantry. His attack succeeded and his troops held an important hill and managed to hold off strong enemy

Martin Bieber entered Army service in March 1917 with Fusilier Regiment 39, was wounded in December and was commissioned as a *Leutnant* while recovering in hospital. He left the Army in 1920, returning fourteen years later with the rank of *Hauptmann* as company commander from October 1935 while attached to the 6th Infantry Division. In October he was transferred to Infantry Regiment 39, where he remained until November 1938, serving as ordnance officer with Infantry Regiment 26 in Flensburg. A few weeks after the outbreak of the Second World War he was transferred into the 86th Infantry Division under the command of *Generalmajor* Joachim Witthoft, seeing action on the Saar Front as part of the XXIII. Army Corps.

counter-attacks. Eventually the division managed to send in reserves to help his regiment, which had been weakened by heavy losses over the course of the day. The personal bravery of Bieber gave the Battle Group the confidence and momentum to carry out a final attack on 5 July, which saw some really hard fighting, and four days later Bieber was wounded by a gun shot through his pelvis.

On 18 January 1940 Bieber had been made Commander of the II. Battalion of Infantry Regiment 167, being promoted to *Major* the following month, and from May he took part in the French campaign, remaining on occupation duty after the French surrender.

Knight's Cross with Oakleaves: Awarded on 2 September 1944, to become the 566th recipient as *Oberst* and *Führer* of Division Grenadier 86, part of Corps Battalion E (XX. Army Corps), for his personal bravery and leadership during the successful breakout of the Brest-Litovsk Pocket. He was personally presented with the Oakleaves by *Reichsführer-SS* Heinrich Himmler in Posen on 7 November 1944. He later saw action in Holland and in December the division was sent to Hungary, where he saw action in Stuhlweissenburg, Budapest and Gran. Bieber was promoted to *Generalmajor* in January 1945, and by April his command was almost surrounded by the Soviet Army in Budapest. He ordered a breakout but it was useless and by early May the Germans had been completely surrounded and trapped. On 13 May Bieber was taken prisoner by Soviet forces, spending ten years in a Soviet prison.

<u>Walter</u> Kurt Gustav SCHILLING
Generalleutnant

* 23 December 1892, Kulm, West Prussia
+ 21 July 1943, Doljenjaja, Ukraine

Knight's Cross: Awarded posthumously on 28 July 1943 as *Generalleutnant* and Commander of the 17th Panzer Division, part of the 1st Panzer Army, for actions near Kursk on the Russian Front. Schilling had not been in command for five weeks when he was killed in action in Doljenjaja near Isjum in Ukraine. He had previously served as a staff officer and had been described by his superiors as 'an excellent officer', however his abilities as a field commander are difficult to judge due to the short time he spent at the front.

Walter Schilling joined the Royal Prussian Army in May 1914 and with the start of the First World War he was attached to the 4th Company of Pioneer Battalion 26. He was commissioned as a *Leutnant* in January 1915 and remained with this battalion throughout the war. He stayed with the Army after the war and from 1933 was attached to the Defence Ministry and the Army Office. At the start of the Second World War he was Chief of Operations in the General Staff of the 8th Army in Poland.

Karl HENKE
Generalmajor

* 22 July 1896, Berlin-Charlottenburg
+ 27 April 1945, South Neutief, East Prussia

Knight's Cross: Awarded on 4 August 1943 as *Oberst* and Commander of the Motorised Engineer Landing Regimental Staff 770 for his organisational talent and diplomatic flair during inter-service rivalry. He was presented with the award by the Commander of Western Tauria [Crimea], *General der Infanterie* Sigismund von Förster. From early 1943 Henke was appointed tactical commander of all Army and German Naval units tasked with supplying the Kuban Bridgehead area via the Kerch Strait. He was promoted to *Generalmajor* in October 1944 while serving as Higher Landing Engineer Leader and from January 1945 he was General of Engineers with Army High Command 4. In April he was caught in the encirclement of Baltiysk near Kaliningrad by Soviet troops and he held his position during close combat fighting for the next few days. On 27 April he shot himself with his last remaining bullet when Soviet forces tried to overrun his position.

Karl Henke joined the Army in August 1914 as a war volunteer with Pioneer Battalion 28 and was wounded in June 1915. He later served as a platoon leader and was commissioned as a *Leutnant* in February 1916, staying with the same unit throughout the war. He remained in the Army after the war, was promoted to *Hauptmann* in February 1931 and served as an engineer of Pioneer Instruction and Test Battalion 1 from October 1935.

Erich-Otto SCHMIDT
Generalmajor

* 17 August 1899, Annaberg, Saxony
+ 18 June 1959, Bühlertal, Baden-Württemberg

Knight's Cross: Awarded on 4 August 1943 as *Oberst* and Commander of Grenadier Regiment 679 while attached to the 333rd Infantry Division for action in the southern sector of the Soviet Union. He took part in the Donets and Kharkov battles as part of the 1st Panzer Army. However, by 2 November 1943 the division had suffered so many casualties that it was downgraded to Division Group 333. From January 1944 Schmidt served as commander of the training staff at the Infantry School at Döberitz and in July he took over as commander of the 1136th Grenadier Brigade. From November he was commander of the 352nd *Volksgrenadier* Division and saw action in the Flensburg area of Schleswig-Holstein in northern Germany, where he was seriously wounded on 23 December 1944. He was promoted to *Generalmajor* while recovering but never returned to combat. He was captured by Us troops in May 1945, being released in June 1947.

Erich-Otto Schmidt joined the Army in 1919 and after his training was assigned to Saxony Infantry Regiment 10 the following year. He was commissioned as a *Leutnant* in March 1924, serving with the regiment for the next ten years and rising to the rank of *Hauptmann*. At the start of the Second World War he was an adjutant with Infantry Regiment 52 with the rank of *Major* and saw action during the opening phase of the invasion of Poland.

Otto-Joachim LÜDECKE
Generalleutnant

* 27 May 1894, Stassfurt, Saxony
+ 13 February 1971, Hassel, Lower Saxony

Knight's Cross: Awarded on 8 August 1943 as *Generalmajor* and Commander of the 56th Infantry Division of the XXXV. Army Corps for his outstanding performance in the battles near Orel on the Russian Front. Lüdecke later saw action during the Battle of Kursk in July 1943, where his division suffered heavy casualties. From September he served as General commanding the engineers of Army Group Centre and was promoted to *Generalleutnant* a month later. In March 1944 he left the front when he was taken ill. On 19 April he was appointed Commander of the 264th Infantry Division and served on the Dalmatian coast, where he fought partisans until 29 April when his car hit a mine and he was seriously wounded. His driver and adjutant died in the explosion. Lüdecke returned to duty in August as commandant of the fortifications in Military District XX, Danzig, and from March 1945 he served in a similar capacity with Military District IV in Dresden. From 11 April he commanded a makeshift unit known as Division Lüdecke and served with *Fallschirm-Panzer Korps Hermann Goring*. In May he surrendered his command to US troops and was later handed over to the British and released on 5 March 1948.

Otto-Joachim Lüdecke entered the Army in September 1913 and was severely wounded early in the war on 27 August 1914, returning to duty in November 1915, but he was wounded once again in May three years later. He stayed in the Army after the war, serving as an engineer with Pioneer Battalion 3 from April 1935 with the rank of *Major*. He was promoted to *Oberst* in March 1940 and later that year served with the XVIII. Army Corps in France.

<u>Rudolf</u> August DEMME
Generalmajor

* 3 June 1894, Mühlhausen, Thuringia
+ 5 January 1975, Meckenheim in North Rhine-Westphalia

Knight's Cross: Awarded on 14 August 1943 as *Oberst* and Commander of Panzer Grenadier Regiment 59 while attached to the 20th Panzer Division for actions near Vasil'yevskoy in the Soviet Union. On the evening of 17 July 1943 Battle Group *Demme* was ordered to pull out of position and move along to the Vasil'yevskoy, where his forces engaged a large Soviet contingent. When they arrived it was obvious that Soviet forces had taken the town and a counter-attack was led by *Oberst* Demme. During the fighting his courage and bravery in battle was an inspiration to his troops and as a result the Soviets were pushed back from the area. Later Demme lost all contact with his division and decided to act on his own initiative, organising his forces to counter-attack using riflemen and panzer forces. He was seen leading from the front and standing on a tank shouting orders – he was the motivation his soldiers needed. By 0600 hours the following morning the area the Germans had been fighting over was theirs, and it was the swift decisiveness of Demme that brought victory.

Knight's Cross with Oakleaves: He became the 537th recipient on 28 July 1944 as *Oberst* and Commander of Panzer Grenadier Regiment 59 for his actions and bravery while leading the armoured elements of his division during the Soviet breakthrough at Bobruisk between 24 June and 4 July 1944. His mission was to proceed northwards and link up with other friendly forces that were trying to break out to the north-west, and after an attack on a small Soviet force he realised that more enemy forces were in the area. The Oakleaves were personally presented to Demme by Hitler at Führer Headquarters in Rastenburg in early August 1944. From 26 September until 6 December he was named as leader of the 17th Panzer Division and on 1 March 1945 he was promoted to *Generalmajor* and named as Commander of the 132nd Infantry Division. He saw action during the

Rudolf Demme joined the Army in September 1914 as a war volunteer and was attached to the Engineer Replacement Battalion II. Commissioned as a *Leutnant* in September 1917, he later saw service in a mortar company and a platoon leader. Demme left the Army after the war, re-joining in January 1937 as an instructor with the rank of *Oberleutnant*. From 1940 he served as an engineer with Replacement Battalion 208 and later as part of the 20th Panzer Division with the rank of *Major*.

terrible battles in the Courland Pocket. Demme surrendered to Soviet troops in May 1945 and spent just over ten years in a Soviet prison camp, being released in October 1955.

Helmut Max STAEDKE
Generalleutnant

* 30 August 1905, Munich, Bavaria
+ 3 September 1973, Tübingen

Knight's Cross: Awarded on 14 August 1943 as *Oberst im Generalstab* and Chief of the General Staff of the XXXV. Army Corps as part of the 2nd Panzer Army for actions in Orel on the Russian Front. He saw action at the beginning of the Kursk offensive from July 1943 while under the command of *General der Infanterie* Lothar Rendulic. From October 1943 he served as Chief of the General Staff of the 9th Army while under the command of *Generaloberst* Walther Model and saw action on the Eastern Front as part of Army Group Centre. He was promoted to *Generalmajor* in April 1944, and attended the 17th Divisional Leaders Course in Neutstadt from mid-February 1945. On 20 April 1945 he was promoted to *Generalleutnant* and six days later was named commander of

Helmut Staedke, seen here as an *Oberst* wearing his Knight's Cross as Chief of the General Staff of the XXXV. Army Corps. He entered the Army in 1924 and served with Artillery Regiment 7, where he remained for nine years.

Staedke is seen here as *Generalmajor* and Chief of the General Staff of the 9th Army.

the 198th Infantry Division, seeing action in Palatinate. On 28 April, just two days after he took command, remnants of the division were taken prisoner by the Americans in Weilheim in Bavaria.

<u>Otto</u> August Wilhelm WÖHLER
General der Infanterie

* 12 July 1894, Grossburgwedel, Hannover
+ 5 February 1987, Grossburgwedel, Hannover

Knight's Cross: Awarded on 14 August 1943 as *General der Infanterie* and Commanding General of the I. Army Corps for his successful leadership during the third battle south of Lake Ladoga, near Leningrad, in mid-1943. From 22 July until 6 August his command, with *Luftwaffe* support, pushed back the assaults made by the Soviet 8th and 67th Soviet armies that were trying to break through the German lines. On 16 August Wöhler took over the leadership of the 8th Army, which had been engaged in a fighting withdrawal from southern Ukraine since late 1943.

Knight's Cross with Oakleaves: He became the 671st recipient on 28 November 1944 as *General der Infanterie* and as Commander-in-Chief of the 8th Army in recognition of his leadership and success while defeating two Soviet attempts to break into Romania in the spring of 1944. The fighting began on 26 April 1944 and the attempted breakthrough by the

Otto Wöhler entered the Army in February 1913, being commissioned the following year as a *Leutnant* while serving as a company leader. He stayed in the Army after the war, serving as a battalion leader and battalion adjutant until April 1924 and then later with various infantry regiments. In June 1935 he was promoted to *Oberstleutnant* while serving as Chief of Operations of the 8th Infantry Division. At the start of the Second World War he was Chief of Operations of the 14th Army, seeing action in Poland. Wöhler was appointed Chief of the General Staff of the 11th Army from October 1940 and from June 1941 saw action during the invasion of the Soviet Union.

Soviets with twenty rifle and several tank divisions failed. According to German reports, 'the Bolshevik enemy suffered heavy personnel losses as well as material loss of 386 tanks, ninety-two guns and one hundred aircraft'. In just three weeks his army had defeated the Soviets in the south-eastern part of Hungary and from December he became the Commander-in-Chief of Army Group South. On 8 May 1945 Wöhler surrendered to the Allies and was later investigated and implicated in the crimes of the *Einsatzgruppen*, the mobile units that executed Jews. He was tried by a US Military Tribunal at Nuremberg from November 1947 and denied knowledge of the *Einsatzgruppen* and any complicity in helping to carry out their actions. He was found guilty of war crimes that included deportations of civilians for slave labour and was sentenced to eight years' imprisonment in October 1948. The following year his sentence was reviewed and based on it being backdated to 1945 he was released in February 1951.

Siegmund Freiherr von SCHLEINITZ
Generalleutnant

+ 23 July 1890, Berlin
+ 30 November 1968, Kiel

Knight's Cross: Awarded on 14 August 1943 as *Generalleutnant* and Commander of the 9th Infantry Division as part of the 17th Army for actions in the Soviet Union. He led his division during the battles at Novorossiysk and in the Kuban, as well as at Melitopol in Ukraine and in the Nikopol Bridgehead. Towards the end of November 1943 he took over as commander of the 361st Infantry Division

Siegmund Freiherr von Schleinitz entered the Prussian Army in September 1909 and later served as a company officer. Commissioned as a *Leutnant* in March 1911, he became adjutant of the III. Battalion of Reserve Infantry Regiment 64 in 1914. He ended the war as a staff officer with the rank of *Hauptmann* and remained in the Army. From October 1935 he served as adjutant of the General Command of the II. Army Corps in Stettin with the rank of *Oberstleutnant*. He later commanded Infantry Regiment 48 during the opening stages of the Second World War in Poland.

in Denmark and from March 1944 he saw action in the Battle of Ternopol in the Soviet Union. From May until September he spent time in the Reserves before being assigned as commander of the Command Staff of the Alps Region. From October he took over from *Generalleutnant* Hubert Stenzel as commander of Division No. 402 in Stettin but was not mobilised for front-line action until January 1945 when Pomerania was invaded by the Soviets. He saw action in the Siege of Kolberg in February and March, until on 15 March he was taken prisoner by the Soviets and remained in custody until his release in October 1955.

Vollrath LÜBBE
Generalleutnant

* 4 March 1894, Klein Lunow, Germany
+ 4 April 1964, Hannover

Knight's Cross: Awarded on 17 August 1943 as *Generalleutnant* and Commander of the 2nd Panzer Division while attached to the XXXXVII. Panzer Corps for actions in the Soviet Union. His division took part in the defensive fighting in the Rzhev Salient in the central sector of the Russian Front. From late 1943 he took part in the Rzhev withdrawal and saw heavy action during the battles of Kursk and Orel, where his command suffered heavy casualties. From February until April 1944, he was attached to the *Führer* Reserves, taking command briefly of the 81st Infantry Division as he was taken ill in June 1944. By early October he had recovered and was briefly made commander of the 462nd *Volksgrenadier* Division in north-east France and for about a month he also was Commandant

Vollrath Lübbe entered the Army in March 1912 and was commissioned as a *Leutnant* two years later while serving with Infantry Regiment 103. He stayed in the Army after the war and from January 1935 served as tactics instructor at the War School in Dresden with the rank of *Major*. In 1937 he served with his old regiment, Infantry Regiment 103, as a battalion commander and from October 1938 he was commander of Cavalry Regiment 13, seeing action in the Polish campaign as part of the 5th Panzer Division.

of Metz. In November he took command of the 49th Infantry Division and the following month he took command of Division No. 433 and saw action on the Eastern Front in the Frankfurt Oder area. He was wounded on 2 February 1945 and just three days later was taken prisoner in Brandenburg by Soviet soldiers and taken to Prison Camp No. 27 in Krasnogorsk in Moscow. In June 1950 he was sentenced to twenty-five years' hard labour but on 11 October 1955 he was released under a general amnesty.

Carl HILPERT
Generaloberst

* 12 September 1888, Nuremberg, Bavaria
+ 1 February 1947, Camp Krasnogorsk near Moscow

Knight's Cross: Awarded on 22 August 1943 as *General der Infanterie* and Commanding General of the LIV. Army Corps, part of the 18th Army, for his outstanding leadership on the Russian Front near Volkhov during the summer offensive. Hilpert distinguished himself against overwhelming Soviet forces and proved to be a great commander, but tragedy struck on 30 September 1943 when his eldest son was killed on the Eastern Front. On 1 January 1944 he was appointed Commanding General of the I. Army Corps and continued to see heavy action on the Eastern Front.

Knight's Cross with Oakleaves: He became the 542nd recipient on 8 August 1944 as *General der Infanterie* and Commanding General of the I. Army Corps while attached to the 16th Army in recognition of his leadership and bravery during the Soviet Summer Offensive of 1944. It was during this time that he saved his command from the jaws of defeat,

Carl Hilpert entered the Army in July 1907 with Bavarian Infantry Regiment 14 and served as an adjutant at the start of the First World War. He remained in the Army after the war and from October 1935 he was serving as commander of Infantry Regiment 35 with the rank of *Oberst*. From 1937 he was Chief of the General Staff with various army commands and was promoted to the rank of *Generalleutnant* in November 1940.

leading them from Soviet encirclement near Polotsk and then through difficult terrain to a safe position. He was personally presented with the Oakleaves by Hitler at Führer Headquarters the Wolf's Lair at Rastenburg on 10 August. From 31 August he was delegated with the leadership of the 16th Army on the Eastern Front, seeing heavy action near Riga. Between 18 and 25 January 1945 he was given the temporary leadership of Army Group South and then he was briefly given temporary leadership of Army Group Courland. On 30 January he took over as Commander-in-Chief of the 16th Army, seeing heavy action in the Soviet Union, and from 6 April he was named as Commander-in-Chief of Army Group Courland. On 7 May he was promoted to *Generaloberst*, but the following day he surrendered to the Soviets, remaining in captivity until his release on 24 December 1948. He had been recommended for the Knight's Cross with Oakleaves and Swords for his 'outstanding achievements in battle', but this was never officially authorised.

<u>Friedrich</u> Wilhelm Hermann HOCHBAUM
General der Infanterie

* 7 August 1894, Magdeburg, Saxony
+ 28 January 1955, Prison Camp 5110/48, Volkhov, Soviet Union

Knight's Cross: Awarded on 22 August 1943 as *Generalleutnant* and Commander of the 34th Infantry Division of the XXXV. Army Corps for his remarkable defensive successes in the Soviet Union. He saw action during the many defensive battles in the Orel Salient and subsequent fighting withdrawals to Bryansk, where he distinguished himself during the summer of 1943.

Friedrich Hochbaum entered military service in May 1913 and was commissioned as a *Leutnant* in August the following year, being wounded three months later. He served with Grenadier Regiment 10 throughout most of the war and was once again wounded in June 1918. He remained in the Army after the war and was promoted to *Oberstleutnant* in January 1938. In July 1940 he took command of Infantry Regiment 253, seeing action during the French campaign.

Hochbaum, centre with Knight's Cross, is seen here with his staff and with him is *Oberst* Ferdinand Hippel, commander of Grenadier Regiment 253, who has just been presented with his Knight's Cross by Hochbaum.

Knight's Cross with Oakleaves: He became the 486th recipient on 4 June 1944 as *Generalleutnant* and Commander of the 34th Infantry Division of the VII. Army Corps in recognition of his leadership during the fierce fighting with Soviet forces between the Dnieper and Taganrog. He was personally presented with the Oakleaves on 20 June by Hitler at the Berghof on the Obersalzburg, and shortly after he was given the leadership of the XVIII. Mountain Corps, seeing action in Lapland as part of the 20th Mountain Army. He was promoted to *General der Infanterie* on 1 September 1944 and his command was confirmed. He continued to see action in Lapland until February 1945, when his command moved to West Prussia, where he fought against Soviet troops. Hochbaum surrendered on 8 May 1945 and was held in a Soviet Prison Camp in Volkhov, where he died on 28 January 1945. He is buried today in the Tschernzy Cemetery in Russia, Grave No. 22.

Nikolaus von VORMANN
General der Panzertruppe

* 24 December 1895, Neumark-Löbau, Western Prussia
\+ 26 October 1959, Berchtesgaden, Bavaria

Knight's Cross: Awarded on 22 August 1943 as *Generalleutnant* and Commander of the 23rd Panzer Division while attached to the XXIV. Panzer Corps for his command during the fighting in the Donets and in the retreat to the Mius River in March 1943. It had by this time proved to be an excellent division and during its time in Russia Vormann's command had lost more than 90 per cent of its armour but had destroyed at least six times as many Soviet tanks. He was involved in the Mius withdrawal in the summer of 1943 and was heavily engaged in the battles of the Dnieper Bend that autumn. Towards the end of December he was given the leadership of the XXXXVII. Panzer Corps and saw action in Kremenchug, an industrial area in Ukraine. On 27 June 1944 Vormann was promoted to *General der Panzertruppe* and took over as leader of the 9th Army. It was a brief appointment and in that time he became involved in the suppression of the Warsaw Uprising, although the main responsibility for the massacre of its inhabitants was down to two SS generals. When Vormann took over command of the 9th Army he wrote, 'the 9th Army has virtually ceased to exist … it doesn't have a single battleworthy formation left'. On 5 October he was named as commander of Fortress Area South-east, a definite demotion – in fact he never held another major command. From 4 May 1945 he was named as commandant of Fortress Alpine,

Nikolaus von Vormann entered the Army as a war volunteer in August 1914 and was wounded the following month and again in June 1915. He later served as adjutant to the II. Battalion of Infantry Regiment 26 in Magdeburg and was wounded once again in December 1915. In fact, Vormann was wounded seven times during the war and was awarded the Wound Badge in Gold. He left the Army in November 1920 and returned four years later. By October 1935 he held the rank of *Major* and served as First General Staff Officer with the 20th Infantry Division. He was promoted to *Oberst* in September 1940, serving as Chief of the General Staff of the XXVIII. Army Corps.

a command that really only existed on paper. Within four days he was in US captivity, where he stayed until his release in August 1948.

Eduard Walter Otto <u>Werner</u> FORST
Generalleutnant

* 21 December 1892, Magdeburg, Saxony-Anhalt
+ 3 February 1971, Wiesbaden, Hesse

Knight's Cross: Awarded on 29 August 1943 as *Generalleutnant* and Commander of the 106th Infantry Division for his leadership during heavy fighting along the Donets River in the Kharkov area on the Russian Front. He hastily put together a counter-thrust and marched against the Soviet forces, creating a defensive line that ensured all Soviet breakthrough attempts were crushed.

Knight's Cross with Oakleaves: He became the 407th recipient on 22 February 1944 as *Generalleutnant* and still Commander of the 106th Infantry Division during attacks while defending the crossing on the Dnieper River at the end of September 1943 against overwhelming enemy forces. Later the following month his forces prevented the expansion of an enemy bridgehead on the west bank of the river south-east of Kremenchuk in Ukraine. His division achieved notable success during bitter combat in December and after personally conducting the necessary reconnaissance while under fire he made ready for the attack. He led his command from the front and his troops recaptured two strongly defended enemy villages that had been lost the previous week. He was presented with the Oakleaves by Hitler on 31 May 1944 at the

Werner Forst entered the Army in April 1911 and was commissioned as a *Leutnant* a year later while attached to Field Artillery Regiment 15. He later transferred to the General Staff of the 7th Cavalry Division and was promoted to *Oberleutnant* in November 1917. He stayed with the Army after the war and by October 1937 had risen to the rank of *Oberstleutnant* and was serving as commander of Artillery Regiment 76. He was promoted to *Oberst* in August 1939 and went on to serve as Artillery Commander 146 from January 1941.

Berghof on the Obersalzburg. On 1 June he was named as Inspector of Artillery with the Commander of the Replacement Army, *Generaloberst* Friedrich Fromm. Forst was captured by US troops on 9 May 1945 and remained a prisoner of war until his release in June 1947.

Wolfgang von KLUGE
Generalleutnant

* 5 May 1892, Stettin, Pomerania
+ 30 October 1976, Kiel, Schleswig-Holstein

Knight's Cross: Awarded on 29 August 1943 as *Generalleutnant* and Commander of the 292nd Infantry Division while attached to Army Group Centre near Orel in the Soviet Union. He was wounded on 20 July 1943 and spent time in hospital before returning to duty in December as Commander of the newly established 357th Infantry Division. It was established in the Radom Area of Poland and from April 1944 was attached to the 4th Panzer Army on the Eastern Front, seeing action during the heavy engagements near Kovel and Tarnopol and in southern Poland. In June Kluge took command of Division 408 for just two weeks before being appointed Commander of the 226th Infantry Division, which was formed from the remnants of the 111th Infantry Division, which had been destroyed at Sevastopol in April. Kluge took it over at Dunkirk, where it remained at battle group strength and from July became Commandant of the area. In September, Kluge took command of fortress Dunkirk form *Oberst* Christian Wittsatt but just two days later he was relieved of his command by Vizeadmiral

Wolfgang von Kluge was the brother of Generalfeldmarschall Günther von Kluge, who committed suicide after the failure of the plot to kill Hitler in July 1944. Wolfgang entered the Army in March 1912 and stayed with the Army after the war. From October 1940 he was commander of Artillery Regiment 31 with the rank of *Oberst* and took part in the invasion of the Soviet Union in June 1941.

Friedrich Frisus, who told him that he had been ordered to evacuate Kluge and his staff and take over Dunkirk himself. On 19 September Kluge and his staff were evacuated from Dunkirk in four torpedo boats and Kluge entered the Reserves. On 31 December 1944 he retired from the army due mainly to political reasons. It was probably because his brother, *Generalfeldmarschall* Günther von Kluge, who had committed suicide, was part of the 20 July 1944 plot to kill Hitler.

Joachim-Friedrich 'Fritz' LANG
Generalmajor

* 14 September 1899, Montigny, Lorraine
+ 16 April 1945, Lochstädter Wald near Pillau, Eastern Prussia

Knight's Cross: Awarded on 4 September 1943 as *Oberst* and Commander of Grenadier Regiment 481 of the 256th Infantry Division for actions during the Battle of Smolensk on the Russian front, where it suffered heavy losses. Lang was personally presented with the Knight's Cross by the commander of the 256th Infantry Division, *Generalleutnant* Paul Danhauser. At the end of June 1944 he took over as commander of Division Group 95 and was promoted to *Generalmajor* on 1 October. On 19 October he took over as Commander of the 95th Infantry Division and saw heavy action near Memel, where the unit was almost destroyed and had to be evacuated by the Navy to Samland. Now at only battle group strength, it faced strong Soviet forces in East Prussia and was trapped and destroyed on 16 April 1945, that same day Lang was killed in action near Lochstädter Wald, Pillau.

Joachim-Friedrich Lang entered the Army in March 1918, serving with Fusilier Regiment 36 and being commissioned as a *Leutnant* in August 1919. He left the Army in December 1920 and re-joined seventeen years later. At the beginning of the Second World War in September 1939 he served as *Hauptmann* with Infantry Regiment 435 and in December 1940 he was battalion commander with Infantry Regiment 380 in France.

<u>Oldwig</u> Otto Wilhelm Gneomar von NATZMER
Generalleutnant

* 29 June 1904, Liegnitz, Silesia
+ 1 April 1980, Dissen am Teutoburgr Wald, Lower Saxony

Knight's Cross: Awarded on 4 September 1943 as *Oberst im Generalstab* and Operations Officer (Ia) of Panzer Grenadier Division *Grossdeutschland* of the XXIII. Army Corps for actions around Okhtyrka in Ukraine and near the Vorskla River in the Soviet Union. On the morning of 15 August, Natzmer led

Oldwig von Natzmer joined the Army in May 1925, was assigned to Mounted Regiment 9 and was commissioned as a *Leutnant* three years later. He was an instructor at the War School in Hannover from February 1935 and was assigned to the General Staff with the Army Transport Department from November 1938. In August the following year he became Chief of the Transport Office and from April 1941 he was Chief of Operations of the 161st Infantry Division with the rank of *Major*.

Oberst Natzmer is seen here with *Generalmajor* Hasso von Manteuffel, the commander of the 7th Panzer Division, shortly after being presented with his Knight's Cross.

his Battle Group on a mission to capture the enemy occupied villages of Grün, Bilsk and Kuzemyn in order to cut off and eliminate Soviet forces on the west bank of the Vorskla River. They made a rapid advance with the help of Tiger tanks, which destroyed several Soviet heavy self-propelled guns, and as a result by the evening of 16 August the Battle Group reported success. Natzmer was promoted to *Generalmajor* in July 1944 and was then appointed Chief of the General Staff of Army Group North. From 27 January 1945 he was transferred and appointed Chief of the General Staff of Army Group *Kurland*, and from mid-February he took over as Chief of the General Staff of Army Group Centre under the command of *Generalfeldmarschall* Ferdinand Schörner. On 15 March Natzmer was promoted to *Generalleutnant* and he surrendered to Allied forces near Dresden on 8 May 1945, remaining in Allied captivity until 10 May 1948.

Heinrich RECKE
Generalleutnant

* 25 August 1890, Konitz, Germany
+ 18 August 1943, Kharkov, Ukraine

Knight's Cross: Awarded posthumously on 4 September 1943 as *Generalleutnant* and Commander of the 161st Infantry Division while attached to the XXXXII. Army Corps for actions in the southern zone of the Eastern Front after the fall of Stalingrad. His division saw action in Kharkov, where it sustained heavy losses and was reduced to battle group strength. Recke personally led an assault group attempting to regain the Soviet village of Panskaja on 15 August 1943. Shortly after the attack began at 3pm he was seen surrounded by five Soviet troops locked in close combat. He was presumably killed and is officially listed as missing in action.

Heinrich Recke entered the Army with Fusilier Regiment 34 in Stettin in March 1909 and from January 1914 he served as adjutant of the II. Battalion with the rank of *Leutnant*. Promoted to *Oberleutnant* in February 1915, he later served as adjutant of the 6th Infantry Brigade and was wounded in January 1918. Later that same year he served as adjutant of the 90th Reserve Infantry Brigade. He remained with the Army after the war and served as commander of Infantry Regiment 466 from August 1939 with the rank of *Oberst*.

<u>Heinrich-Walter</u> Wilhelm Ernst Wiwigens Konrad BRONSART VON SCHELLENDORFF
Generalmajor

* 21 September 1906, Neustrelitz, Mecklenburg-Strelitz,
+ 22 September 1944, near Château-Salins in Lorraine, France

Knight's Cross: Awarded on 10 September 1943 as *Oberst* and Commander of Panzer Grenadier Regiment 13 of the 5th Panzer Division for his distinguished leadership near Orel against a strong Soviet force north-west of Katunayak. As part of the 5th Panzer Division, Bronsart von Schellendorff took part in the unsuccessful Kursk offensive and the withdrawal near Rzhev, and later near Demjansk and on the middle Dnieper in late 1943.

Knight's Cross with Oakleaves: Awarded on 12 February 1944 to become the 394th recipient as *Oberst* and Commander of Panzer Grenadier Regiment 13 while still attached to the 5th Panzer Division for his bravery and leadership during the defensive actions north of Kalinkawitschy in January 1944. The Soviet forces sought to crush the bridgehead there from the north and cut off the German troops, and then managed to push back Bronsart von Schellendorff's weaker forces. However, the German forces managed to keep open the escape road until all units had succeeded in evacuating the area. The division's retreat route was later blocked by Soviet soldiers and Bronsart von Schellendorff, acting swiftly, assembled a fighting force that consisted mainly of his divisional staff to push back the enemy troops and reopen the road. From May he served as appointed Chief Personnel Officer with the General Staff of Army Command 8 and later attended the Divisional Leaders Course in Hirschberg. From 4 September he served as Commander of Panzer Brigade 111, seeing action on the Western Front where on the 22nd he was severely wounded in combat near Weisskirchen. He was evacuated to a field hospital near Château-Salins in Lorraine, France, where he later died.

Heinrich-Walter Bronsart von Schellendorff entered the Army as a volunteer in April 1924 and was attached to Mounted Regiment 6. He later served as adjutant and squadron commander, rising to the rank of *Rittmeister* in October 1935. From November 1939 he served as commander of Reconnaissance Battalion 36, part of the 36th Infantry Division, while seeing action in Luxembourg and France in 1940. He continued to serve with the same division for the next few years and was promoted to *Oberstleutnant* in February 1943.

Martin Friedrich Karl UNREIN
Generalleutnant

* 1 January 1901, Weimar, Thuringia
+ 22 January 1972, Munich, Bavaria

Knight's Cross: Awarded on 10 September 1943 as *Oberst* and Commander of Panzer Grenadier Regiment 4 of the 6th Panzer Division for his successful leadership during the aftermath of the Battle of Kursk. It was awarded primarily for his part in the fighting at Alexejevka in July 1943 and during the fourth battle of Kharkov on 23 August 1943. There, with only seven tanks at his disposal, his regiment fought for six hours against a strong Soviet fighting force. His actions prevented the Soviets from advancing further and in doing so prevented a German catastrophe. On 30 October 1943 Unrein took command of the 14th Panzer Division and was promoted to *Generalmajor* on 1 January 1944, later seeing action at Krivoy Rog, Kirovograd and in the Dnieper battles.

Knight's Cross with Oakleaves: He became the 515th recipient on 26 June 1944 as *Generalmajor* and Commander of the 14th Panzer Division while attached to the III. Army Corps for continued actions on the Russian Front. This included his part in the Battle of Kirovograd between 5 and 22 January 1944 and the defensive battles at Cherkassy

Martin Unrein entered the Army in March 1918 and was commissioned as a *Leutnant* four years later while serving with Mounted Regiment 7. From October 1936 he served as tactics instructor at the War School in Dresden and later served as adjutant with the XI. Army Corps. From January 1940 he served as commander of Reconnaissance Battalion 268, seeing action on the Maginot Line from June that year. From mid-1941, now with the rank of *Oberstleutnant*, he served with the 6th Panzer Division.

between late January and March 1944. In mid-May he took part in the fierce fighting near the Dniester River against a large Soviet force where his troops almost destroyed the Soviet 8th Guard Army and captured all of their artillery. Shortly after being awarded with the Oakleaves Unrein was promoted to *Generalleutnant* and in early September 1944 he became ill and was hospitalised. He returned to his panzer division on 25 November and took part in the fierce fighting in the Courland area. From February 1945 he took command of the III. SS-Panzer Corps before being given command of Panzer Division *Clausewitz* in April, seeing action in the area around Braunschweig, Magdeburg, in Germany. During the last days of the war his command attempted to rescue Berlin, which had been surrounded by the Soviets, but this failed and they had to retreat. His division raised considerable havoc in the Allied rear and its troops mainly consisted of young men and boys who still believed in Hitler and Nazism. Finally, on 24 April 1945, Unrein surrendered his division to the Americans and he went into captivity, being released in mid-1947.

Ernst KÖNIG
Generalmajor

* 12 May 1908, Fulda, Thuringia
+ 3 March 1986, Göttingen, Lower Saxony

Knight's Cross: Awarded on 16 September 1943 as *Major* and Leader of Grenadier Regiment 12 as part of the 31st Infantry Division for actions on the Russian Front. On 10 August König and his regiment were south of Dmitrovsky, near Moscow, when he decided to take up the defence of the city and in doing so prevented the swift capture by Soviet troops. This was an excellent move by König as this helped in the planned withdrawal by the XXXXVI. Panzer Corps from the area. Late on 27 August his regiment became encircled in the area of Borissow-Lemeschok and his command held the front against eighteen hostile tanks with infantry. In total König and his men were able to hold out for almost two days despite the intense close combat and the loss of their anti-tank weapons and almost all of their officers. König was promoted to *Oberstleutnant* in October 1943 and saw action in the northern sector of the Russian front, fighting at Demjansk. There, in April 1944, König was promoted to the rank of *Oberst*.

Ernst König served with the police from May 1927, transferred into the Army in October 1935 and was commissioned as a *Leutnant* in May 1939. From September he served as commander of the I. Battalion of Infantry Regiment 82 and saw action in Poland, France, Belgium and later in the Soviet Union – being promoted to *Major* in February 1942.

Knight's Cross with Oakleaves: He became the 598th recipient on 21 September 1944 as *Oberst* and Commander of Grenadier Regiment 12, part of the 14th Infantry Division, for continued actions on the Russian Front. In early July his division conducted a desperate retreat near Swislatsch, south-east of Minsk, and then further via Grodno in Belarus by 8 July, and finally saw action in the area around Gołdap near Poland. Throughout the summer of 1944 he led his regiment and for six days he briefly commanded the 31st Infantry Division, where his command suffered heavy casualties. He proved a capable and brave regimental commander and saved many soldiers from the Minsk Pocket during the retreat. From 20 November he took command of the 28th *Jäger* Division. He saw action in East Prussia during the last few months of the war and was promoted to *Generalmajor* on 30 January 1945. He was seriously wounded in March of that year and was evacuated to hospital. He was still in hospital when Germany surrendered and remained in Allied captivity until 1 September 1947.

Dr jur. Hans BOELSEN
Generalleutnant

* 6 March 1894, Emden, Hanover
+ 24 October 1960, Frankfurt am Main

Knight's Cross: Awarded on 17 September 1943 as *Oberst* and Commander of Panzer Grenadier Regiment 111 while attached to the 11th Panzer Division for actions during the 4th Panzer Armies' withdrawal west of Belgorod. On 17 August Soviet forces succeeded in achieving a broad penetration of the German front line to the north, and the following day this was expanded to the south and west, creating an immediate threat to the XXIV. Panzer Corps. Boelsen was informed of the gravity of the situation and

Hans Boelsen entered the Army in August 1914 as a war volunteer with Grenadier Regiment 110, being commissioned as a *Leutnant* the following year. He was wounded in 1915 and after he had recovered he served as platoon leader but was shortly after taken ill and hospitalised. He ended the war with the 24nd Infantry Division and left the Army in October 1920 to study law. He re-joined in July 1934 and served as company commander and later as tactics instructor at the War School in Potsdam with the rank of *Major*.

without waiting for orders he led his regiment in a counter-thrust to the east and marched towards enemy positions. On the way his regiment gathered up stragglers from other commands and took part in some fierce fighting and so assumed leadership of what became a large battle group. His actions pushed back enemy forces and his brave and ruthless actions made on his own initiative consequently prevented the enemy's attack, which allowed the Panzer Corps to complete its planned operations. Boelsen later attended the 8th Divisional Leaders course in Döberitz, and from 5 March 1944 he was given the leadership of the 29th Grenadier Division. From April until May he took over as leader of the 26th Panzer Division and in June was promoted to *Generalmajor*. From September took command of the 18th Panzer Grenadier Division, seeing action on the Eastern Front. In March 1945 he was promoted to *Generalleutnant* and served as Commander of Special Purpose Division 172, serving on the northern coast of the Netherlands until the end of the war. Boelsen surrendered to Allied troops in March 1945 and remained in captivity until his release on 30 June 1947.

Dr phil. Johannes SCHULZ
Generalmajor

* 23 October 1892, Kaltenborn, Jüterbog
+ 27 November 1943, Vasylivka, Kirovograd

Knight's Cross: Awarded on 19 September 1943 as *Oberst* and Commander of Panzer Grenadier Regiment 10 of the 9th Panzer Division for actions during the Battle of Kursk in the Soviet Union. From May 1943 he took over the leadership of the panzer division and saw heavy combat in the southern sector of the front during the

Johannes Schulz served in the First World War as a platoon leader and as a company leader with the rank of *Oberleutnant*. Leaving the Army in 1925, he re-joined ten years later and was assigned to the Staff of Engineer Battalion 21 with the rank of *Major*. He later served as Commander of Engineer Battalion 29 and was promoted to *Oberst* in January 1942 while attached to the Staff of the General of Engineers and Fortresses in the High Command of the Army.

retreat to the Mius, in the Battles of Stalino and in Zaporozhye in October. Schulz was killed in action near Vasylivka in Kirovograd on 27 November 1943 and was posthumously promoted to the rank of *Generalmajor*. He is buried in the German War Cemetery, Block 12, Row 3, Grave 162 at Kirovograd in Ukraine.

Peter KÖRTE
Generalmajor

* 26 June 1896, Berlin
+ 13 January 1947, Bielefeld

Knight's Cross: Awarded on 27 September 1943 as *Oberst* and Commander of Füsilier Regiment 26 while attached to the 30th Infantry Division for actions at Staraja Russa and in Leningrad. He was attached to the Commander-in-Chief West briefly as a divisional commander from 9 October until October 1944. He then took command of the 49th Infantry Division, which was withdrawn from front-line duty just a week later, and from 7 November he took command of the 246th Volksgrenadier Division. He had taken over from *Oberst* Gerhard Wick, who had surrendered most of the division to the Americans in late October 1944. Remnants of the division and other units, which included the remnants of the defunct 49th Infantry Division, were pulled together and this brought its strength up to 11,141 men. Körte took his new command into action at Aachen in November and was heavily involved in the Battle of the Huertgen Forest. On 1 January 1945 Körte was promoted to *Generalmajor* but the following day he reported sick and was sent to hospital in Schneidemühl in Poland. He was then transferred to a hospital in Hamburg the following month. He was still in hospital when he went into British captivity on 5 May 1945 and he died in January 1947.

Peter Körte was a war volunteer from December 1914, was attached to Guard Regiment 3 and was later transferred into Reserve Infantry Regiment 53. When the war ended he transferred to the Police in January 1922, returning to the ranks of the Army in October 1935 with the rank of *Hauptmann*. From October 1936 he served as company commander with Infantry Regiment 25 and from September 1941 he served with Infantry Regiment 26, part of the 30th Infantry Division, in the Soviet Union.

Helmuth HUFFMANN
Generalleutnant

* 31 July 1891, Werden an der Ruhr, Rhine Province
+ 9 December 1975, Bad Godesberg, North Rhine-Westphalia

Knight's Cross: Awarded on 30 September 1943 as *Generalleutnant* and Commander of the 62nd Infantry Division, part of the XXX. Army Corps, for actions during the latter stages of the Kursk Offensive and in the withdrawal from the Dniester region. From mid-December Huffmann was named commander of the newly reformed 277th Infantry Division after it had been disbanded following the fall of France in 1940. Its men, mostly from older age groups, had then returned to their civilian life. In February 1944 it was ready for front-line duty and was transported to Narbonne in southern France, where Huffmann took up his command. In May he was assigned to the Staff of Artillery School I in Berlin and from 27 May he was named its commander. He surrendered to the Allies on 8 May 1945 and remained in captivity until mid-1947.

Edmund HOFFMEISTER
Generalleutnant

* 4 March 1898, Aschaffenburg, Bavaria
+ 20 February 1951, Prison Camp Nr. 476, Asbest-Sverdlovsk,
Soviet Union

Knight's Cross: Awarded on 6 October 1943 as *Generalmajor* and Commander of the 383rd Infantry Division while attached

Edmund Hoffmeister entered the Army in August 1912 with Infantry Regiment 30, being commissioned as a *Leutnant* two years later. Wounded at the start of the First World War, he later served as a battalion adjutant and then as an orderly officer. He stayed in the Army after the war and was promoted to *Major* in September 1934 while serving as battalion commander with Infantry Regiment 19. At the start of the Second World War he was serving as commander of Infantry Regiment 21 with the rank of *Oberstleutnant* and saw action during the invasion of France as part of the 17th Infantry Division.

to the 9th Army for his command and bravery on the Russian Front. He saw action at Bryansk, Mogilev and Bobruisk, and was promoted to *Generalleutnant* in March 1944 but remained commander of his infantry division until June. He was then given leadership of the XXXXI. Panzer Corps, replacing *General der Artillerie* Helmuth Weidling, and saw action near Bobruisk in the Soviet Union until 1 July 1944, when he was captured by Soviet forces. When the war ended all information relating to Hoffmeister's imprisonment was sketchy and it was reported that he had been hanged in 1947 in Kiev. Finally the Soviets stated that Hoffmeister had died in Prison Camp No. 476 in Asbest-Sverdlovsk on 20 February 1951, although some sources quote March 1951.

Karl Eduard Friedrich ARNING
Generalmajor

* 10 February 1892, Berlin
+ 17 November 1964, Hamburg-Bramfeld in Lower Saxony.

Knight's Cross: Awarded on 11 October 1943 as *Oberst* and Commander of Grenadier Regiment 24 as part of the 21st Infantry Division in recognition of his leadership on the Eastern Front during the battle for the Sinyarino Heights near Leningrad. His regiment came to prominence when the Soviet 30th Guards Rifle Corps attacked the 21st Infantry Division on 15 September 1943, when they succeeded in the capture of a vital hill. Arning's regiment played a decisive role in pushing back the Soviet force, subsequently halting the Soviet counter-attack. In April he was attached to Army Group North Ukraine as a temporary divisional commander, before taking over as

Karl Arning joined the Army at the age of twenty in September 1912 as a *Fahnenjunker* with Infantry Regiment 20. Commissioned as a *Leutnant* in March 1914, at the beginning of the First World War he was serving as a platoon commander. In May 1917 he was promoted to *Oberleutnant* and was named as ordnance officer with the Staff of 2nd Guards Infantry Brigade. He won both classes of the Iron Cross during the last six months of the war while serving as company commander with Infantry Regiment 20. He left the Army after the war and worked for a bank in Frankfurt and then Bremen before returning to the Army in October 1934.

Commander of the 75th Infantry Division in June 1944. He led his division during the retreat from Siret in north-east Romania to Dniester in Ukraine before being promoted to *Generalmajor* on 1 September. The following month his division saw action in the Carpathians region of Ukraine, where they remained until February 1945. He then withdrew to Upper Silesia. Arning was appointed Battle Commandant and led a combat group while taking part in what was called the 'Prague Offensive' near Moravia-Ostrau. In May he was captured by enemy forces and spent just over ten years in Soviet captivity, being released in October 1955.

<u>Anton</u> Rudolf GLASL
Generalmajor

* 13 February 1897, Freising, Bavaria
+ 7 April 1965, Mühldorf am Inn, Bavaria

Knight's Cross: Awarded on 11 October 1943 as *Oberst* and Commander of Mountain *Jäger* Regiment 100 of the 5th Mountain Division for actions in the Karbussel area of the Soviet Union. On 22 July 1943 Soviet forces, which included three regiments supported by tanks and ground-attack aircraft, attacked elements of the 5th Mountain Division. One of the largest elements was Glasl's Mountain *Jäger* Regiment, which played a major role in pushing back the Russian attacks, mostly in close combat, and it suffered heavy losses to the Soviet forces. On 24 July the Russians attacked again and penetrated three parts of the German defences. Without any support, Glasl mounted a defence and attacked enemy forces, pushing them back

Anton Glasl entered the Army in April 1916 with Bavarian Infantry Regiment 16 and was commissioned as a *Leutnant* the following year. He stayed in the Army after the war, rising to the rank of *Major* in August 1936 while a company commander with Infantry Regiment 20. From October 1937 he served as Chief of Operations on the General Staff of the 10th Division and saw action during the invasion of Poland. In February 1940 he was appointed Chief of Operations on the General Staff of the XIII. Army Corps, now with the rank of *Oberstleutnant*, seeing action during the invasion of France from May 1940.

and thwarting their attack. On 7 August the Russians attacked again and once more in several waves with strong artillery and air support. Every time they were pushed back, suffering heavy losses, however on their final attack they achieved penetration of the German defences. There was now a real danger that Soviet forces could attack from the rear. Glasl rounded up his staff, which included all his communication troops, messengers, cooks and drivers, and put together a makeshift force to fight the Russians. He led the bitter fighting at the front, which ended with the Soviets fleeing and suffering once again heavy losses. Glasl was praised by his commanders and his men, his spirit, personal courage and outstanding bravery inspiring his officers who had repeatedly pushed back the enemy during close combat. He was praised by his commanders and in mid-March he attended the 10th Divisional Leader's course. From July he was attached to the General Staff of the Replacement Command of the XVIII. Army Corps, where he remained until the end of the war. Promoted to *Generalmajor* on 15 February 1945, he surrendered to Allied troops on 9 May and remained in Allied captivity until 30 June 1947.

Kurt LOTTNER
Generalmajor

* 10 October 1899, Hamm, Germany
+ 15 March 1957, Bad Schwartau

Knight's Cross: Awarded on 14 October 1943 as *Oberst* and Commander of Grenadier Regiment 111 of the 35th Infantry Division for actions on the Russian Front. He led his regiment during the withdrawal from Rzhev and was heavily engaged in the defensive fighting on the central sector that summer. In 1944 Lottner was appointed Chief of Staff of the General

Kurt Lottner entered the Army in June 1917 with Infantry Regiment 24 and was commissioned as a *Leutnant* in January 1918. He joined the *Freikorps* after the war and re-entered the Army in 1925. After attending many courses, he was attached to the Army General Staff from October 1935. He was promoted to *Oberstleutnant* in August 1939 and the following month he was appointed Chief of Operations with the 239th Infantry Division, seeing action during the Polish campaign.

of Infantry while attached to the High Command of the Army. He was promoted to *Generalmajor* at the end of January 1945, and from April until May he served as Battle Commandant of Lübeck. On 2 May, as British troops prepared to enter Lübeck, Lottner, together with the Mayor of Lübeck and its police commander Walther Schröder, knew that to put up any resistance to the British 11th Armoured Division was senseless and they ordered the removal of explosive charges from the bridges and harbours around the town. The town was surrendered to British troops on 8 May, and Lottner was transferred to the Island Special Camp 11 in Bridgend, Wales, from January 1946, until his release on 25 November 1947.

Gerhard SCHMIDHUBER

Generalmajor

* 9 April 1894, Dresden, Saxony
+ 11 February 1945, Budapest, Hungary

Knight's Cross: Awarded on 18 October 1943 as *Oberst* and Commander of Panzer Grenadier Regiment 304 of the 2nd Panzer Division for his actions during the defensive fighting in the Dnieper bridgehead west of Lyubech in late September 1943. From early November until mid-December he was also commander of the 2nd Panzer Division and took part in the fighting in Kursk, Orel and at Yelnja and Kiev. From February 1944 he attended the 9th Divisional Leaders Course in Hirschberg and from early May he served briefly on the General Staff of Army Group North Ukraine. He was then appointed acting commander of the 7th Panzer Division and from July 1944 he was acting

Gerhard Schmidhuber was a War Volunteer with the 12th Royal Saxony Infantry Regiment and saw action as a *Leutnant* during the First World War. He left the Army in 1920 but re-joined in July 1934 and served with various regiments, being promoted to *Major* four years later. From August 1939 he served as battalion commander with Infantry Regiment 103 and saw action during the invasion of Belgium and France in 1940.

commander of the 8th Panzer Division in northern Ukraine. From September Schmidhuber took over as commander of the 13th Panzer Division and suffered heavy losses and lost nearly all of his tanks before being withdrawn in October, when he was promoted to *Generalmajor*.

Knight's Cross with Oakleaves: Awarded on 21 January 1945, as the 706th recipient, as *Generalmajor* and Commander of the 13th Panzer Division while attached to the 6th Army for his leadership during the battle of Budapest, where it proved to be one of the hardest-fighting units in the defence of the city. However, most of his division had been encircled in late December and was destroyed when the German garrison tried unsuccessfully to break out of the city on 11 February 1945 – that same day Schmidhuber was killed during the heavy fighting. He is buried today in the German War Cemetery, Block 1 in Budaörs, Hungary.

Richard KOTZ
Generalmajor

* 12 September 1886, Waldau, Baden
+ 8 June 1960, Bad Honnef, North-Rhine Westphalia

Knight's Cross: Awarded on 21 October 1943 as *Oberst* and Commander of Grenadier Regiment 389 while attached to the 217th Infantry Division for actions on the Russian Front. Kotz took over command of his regiment in December 1939 and later saw action during the invasion of France from May 1940. From June 1941 he saw action in

Richard Kotz entered the Army Officers School at Ettlingen in April 1905 and served with Foot Guards Regiment 4 from August 1914. He later served as a platoon and company leader and was awarded a field commission in August 1918 because of his continued bravery. He left the Army in May 1927 and worked as a military adviser in Turkey and then China, entering the German Army in 1934. From August 1939 he served as Commander of Infantry Regiment 389 and was promoted to *Oberstleutnant* in December.

the Soviet Union and took part in the sieges of Oranienburg and Leningrad and later near Volchov. It was while fighting in these areas that he was recognised for his leadership and bravery, being awarded the Knight's Cross. On 26 September 1943 he was wounded and admitted to hospital, where he remained until January 1944 when he was appointed commander of the Weapons School of Army Group C. He was promoted to Generalmajor in December 1944 and from early 1945 he took over as commander of the Weapons School of the Commander-in-Chief South. Kotz surrendered to US troops in May 1945 and remained in captivity until his release on 6 May 1947.

Hanns LAENGENFELDER
Generalmajor

* 8 February 1903, Nuremberg, Bavaria
+ 18 July 1982, Nuremberg, Bavaria

Knight's Cross: Awarded on 21 October 1943 as *Oberstleutnant* and Commander of Grenadier Regiment 106 as part of the 15th Infantry Division for actions on the Russian Front. On the night of 30 September and 1 October 1943 two Soviet regiments had created a bridgehead on the western bank of the Dnieper River west of Dnepropetrovsk. Laengenfelder led his men in a counter-attack of the position and eliminated the Soviet forces on the bridgehead. He was promoted to *Oberst* in November 1943 and remained commander of his regiment until early January 1944, and in October he attended the 14th Divisional Leaders Course in Hirschberg. From 17 October he took over the leadership of the 15th Infantry Division and saw action against Soviet forces once again. In early January 1945 he was promoted to the rank of *Generalmajor* and his command of the 15th Infantry Division was confirmed.

Hanns Laengenfelder entered the Army with Infantry Regiment 21 in April 1923 and was commissioned as a *Leutnant* three years later. He was later attached to the War Academy in Berlin and was promoted to *Hauptmann* in 1935. Four years later he was Transport Commandant in Munich. From July 1940 he was Chief of Operations on the Staff of the Transport Director of Paris with the rank of *Major*. In January 1941 he was Chief Supply Officer with the 31st Infantry Division and saw action from June 1941 in the Soviet Union.

Knight's Cross with Oakleaves: Awarded on 30 April 1945, without a serial number (he would have been the 856th recipient) as *Generalmajor* and Commander of the 15th Infantry Division, part of the XXIX. Army Corps, for continued operations against Soviet forces on the Eastern Front. On 19 February 1945 he led his division and thwarted a Soviet breakthrough attempt by two divisions near Lučenec and Zvolen. On 25 February the Soviets reached the village of Zvolen to find that Laengenfelder held the village and he managed to hold back nine attempts to break through into the sector held by the XXIX. Army Corps. He then took part in heavy action in Slovakia from March, and his division managed to slow the Red Army, which enabled the Germans to bring up their much-needed reserves. He surrendered to Soviet forces on 10 May 1945 and was imprisoned until his release on 10 October 1955, when he returned to Germany.

Kurt Erich CHILL
Generalleutnant

* 1 May 1895, Thorn, West Prussia
+ 5 July 1976, Grömitz, Hamburg-Harburg

Knight's Cross: Awarded on 25 October 1943 as *Generalleutnant* and Commander of the 122nd Infantry Division while attached to the I. Army Corps for actions in the Soviet Union. On 15 October his command attacked Hill 180.3, a position located in the area of Nevel and south of Lake Karachay in the southern Ural mountain area. The attack was a complete success, pressing on beyond its objective to the edge of Lake Karachay, where a Soviet division and brigade were almost destroyed and a large amount of Soviet weaponry was captured. Chill stayed as

Kurt Chill entered the Army in April 1913 and served as platoon and company leader during the First World War while attached to Infantry Regiment 61. He was commissioned as a *Leutnant* in January 1915 and when the war ended he joined the police in Berlin. In October 1935 he re-joined the Army with the rank of *Major* and was attached to Infantry Regiment 65. From December 1940 he served as commander of Infantry Regiment 45 while attached to the 21st Infantry Division.

commander of the division until February 1944, when he entered the Reserves for a brief rest before being appointed Commander of the 85th Infantry Division ten days later. Chill was the first commander of the newly created division and was camping in the rear area of 15th Army in northern France on D-Day on 6 June 1944. He was then sent to Normandy, where in early August his division suffered heavy losses during the fighting in the Falaise Pocket and by August its strength had been reduced. In September Chill saw action against Allied paratroopers in Operation Market Garden, the Allied invasion of Holland. From early December he entered the Reserves and from early February 1945 he was delegated with the leadership of the LV. Army Corps in East Prussia. By the end of the war he had escaped Soviet captivity and was taken prisoner by British troops on 12 May, where he remained until mid-1947.

Ludwig Johann MÜLLER
General der Infanterie

* 28 June 1892, Zeselberg, Germany
+ 28 June 1972, Ettlingen, Germany

Knight's Cross: Awarded on 25 October 1943 as *Generalleutnant* and Commander of the 97th Jäger Division for his leadership during the campaign for the Kuban Bridgehead, and in particular the fighting for Hill 114.1 east of Moldavanskoe between 16 July and 14 September 1943. The Soviets tried many times to seize this important hill from which all their movements could be observed, but all attempts failed. From mid-December Müller served in the Reserves and in early January 1944 he attended a course for commanding generals and was then assigned to the staff of Army Group A.

Ludwig Müller entered the Army as a war volunteer in October 1914 and served as a company leader with Infantry Regiment 22 during the First World War. He remained with the Army after the war and from October 1935 was attached to the Military Economic Department of the Armed Forces in Berlin. He later served as Operations Officer with various different commands and was promoted to *Oberst* in February 1940. From June he served as Chief of the General Staff of the XXIX. Army Corps, seeing action during the invasion of France.

Knight's Cross with Oakleaves: He became the 440th recipient on 6 April 1944 as *Generalleutnant* and Leader of the XXIX. Army Corps for his leadership during the defensive battles as part of the 6th Army in the winter of 1943 and 1944. His corps was present at the fighting retreat in the Nikopol sector as the 6th Army fought to open up an escape route and break through to the west via the Bol'shaya area. Later Müller and his corps launched an attack that secured almost 10 miles of front and captured various towns in the region. In May Müller was promoted to *General der Infanterie* and appointed Commanding General of the XXXXIV. Army Corps, seeing action in Romania. He was presented with the Oakleaves by Hitler at the Obersalzburg in Austria on 20 June 1944 together with *Generalmajor* Gottfried Weber, *General der Artillerie* Ernst-Eberhard Hell, *Generalleutnant* Friedrich Hochbaum, *Generalmajor* Wolf Hagemann and *Oberst* Horst Niemack, who was presented with the Swords. In August his command had come across elements of the 6th Army that had made their way out of Stalingrad and were now heading towards Ukraine close to the area of the Dniester River. Here he picked up more troops and on 21 August, after a failed attempt to break out together with his troops, he was captured by Soviet forces. He remained in Soviet captivity until his release on 9 October 1955, when he could return to Germany.

Franz Karl WESTHOVEN

Generalleutnant

* 7 December 1894, Ludwigshafen, Baden
+ 9 October 1983, Heidelberg, Baden-Württemberg

Knight's Cross: Awarded on 25 October 1943 as *Generalleutnant* and Commander of the 3rd Panzer Division, part of the III. Panzer Corps, for actions during the Battle of Kursk and Belgorod in July and August 1943. His division suffered heavy losses during the fighting in Kharkov and Westhoven remained commander of the division until mid-October 1943, when he entered the Reserves. From February 1944 he was attached to Panzer Group West on special duties and from early March he was given the leadership of the 21st Panzer Division. He was sent to Hungary but only briefly before being sent to Normandy in May 1944. He remained in Normandy, where he was given temporary leadership of the 2nd Panzer Division before entering the Reserves once again. From August he was appointed Deputy General Inspector of Panzer Troops and at the same time he was commander of the Panzer Troops School until the end of the war.

Gerhard WEBER
Generalmajor

* 21 March 1898, Merseburg, Saxony
+ 13 January 1944, south Cherkassy, Ukraine

Knight's Cross: Awarded on 26 October 1943 as *Oberst* and Commander of Motorised Grenadier Regiment 41 of the 10th Panzer Grenadier Division for actions during the Kursk offensive. He took part in the Battle of Kiev towards the end of 1943 and later during the retreat to the Dnieper. He also took part in the heavy fighting in Ukraine. He was killed in action on 13 January 1944 south of Cherkassy in Ukraine and his body disappeared, so he has no known grave. He was posthumously promoted to the rank of *Generalmajor* on 1 January 1944.

Hans KAMECKE
Generalleutnant

* 18 August 1890, Halberstadt, Saxony
+ 16 October 1943, hospital near Kolpen, Soviet Union

Knight's Cross: Awarded posthumously on 27 October 1943 as *Generalleutnant* and Commander of the 137th Infantry Division while attached to the XX, Army Corps for actions on the Russian Front. He took part in trying to rescue the 6th Army at Stalingrad and after the failure his division was moved to the south-west of Orel. Here he took part in heavy defensive fighting and later in the retreat, when his command crossed the Dnieper. His division defended its position near Desná in the Nikolayevsky area between 7 and 17 September 1943. The division was badly under strength after two years of heavy fighting and Soviet units had crossed the Dnieper to face the German division near Krivino. On the morning of

Hans Kamecke entered the Army in March 1909 with Infantry Regiment 26, was commissioned as a *Leutnant* the following year and saw action during the First World War. When the war was over he joined the police, rising to the rank of *Polizei-Oberstleutnant*. In October 1935 he transferred back into the Army, serving as a battalion commander with Infantry Regiment 124.

15 October Kamecke drove to the forward command post of the 447th Infantry Regiment for a battle report. On his return trip to divisional headquarters near Kolpen, his command vehicle was suddenly attacked by Soviet fighters and he was mortally wounded. He died the following day.

Arthur KULLMER
Generalleutnant

* 27 August 1896, Gross Bockenheim, Upper Palatinate
+ 28 March 1953, POW Camp Asbest, Ural

Knight's Cross: Awarded on 27 October 1943 as *Generalleutnant* and Commander of the 296th Infantry Division while attached to the XVIII. Army Corps for his successful leadership during the battles near Orel, Gomel and Bobruisk in Belarus and the Soviet Union. His command was reorganised in the autumn of 1943 but was almost destroyed in June 1944 during the Soviet summer offensive, with Kullmer being one of only a few hundred that was able to retreat to safety. From 15 July he was commander of the 558th Grenadier Division but did not see any action until later in the year, when the division was known as the 558th *Volksgrenadier* Division and saw action in the central sector of the Eastern Front against the Soviets.

Knight's Cross with Oakleaves: He became the 758th recipient on 28 February 1945 as *Generalleutnant* and Commander of the 558th *Volksgrenadier* Division, part of the VII. Army Corps, for his bravery and leadership during the heavy fighting near the Heiligenbeil Pocket in East Prussia. He later fought at Pillau, where his command suffered heavy casualties in East

Arthur Kullmer was a war volunteer with Infantry Regiment 118 from August 1914 and was wounded during action in October 1915. He transferred into Infantry Regiment 7 from early 1916 and was commissioned as a *Leutnant* in July. Two months later he was once again wounded and hospitalised. He stayed with the Army after the war and in October 1935 he served as adjutant of Infantry Regiment 20, being promoted to *Major* in January 1936.

Prussia. On 14 April he was appointed the Commanding General of the XXXXIII. Army Corps, seeing action in Slovakia, where he surrendered to US troops on 8 May 1945. However, he was later handed over to the Soviets and was imprisoned and badly treated, dying on 28 March 1953.

Albert PRAUN
General der Nachrichtentruppe

* 11 December 1894, Bad Staffelstein, Lichtenfels
+ 3 March 1975, Munich

Knight's Cross: Awarded on 27 October 1943 as *Generalleutnant* and Commander of the 129th Infantry Division while attached to the 9th Army for his leadership and success during the defensive battles around Rzhev on the Eastern Front. From early October 1943 he was Signals Officer of Army Group Centre and from April 1944 he was Commander of the 277th Infantry Division while serving in southern France. He later saw action during the Battle of Caen in July 1944 and on 12 August he was appointed Head of the Armed Forces Signals and Communications. He took over from General Erich Fellgiebel, who had been arrested and later executed for his part in the plot to overthrow Hitler. One of his first priorities was to speak with the head of the Reich Security Main Office, *SS-Obergruppenführer* Ernst Kaltenbrunner, and he told him that he should stop arresting members of the signals corps because Germany was losing so many highly skilled and irreplaceable men. Praun told Kaltenbrunner that a shortage of these expert men would soon adversely affect the war effort, and remarkably the SS General agreed and there were no further arrests. Praun was promoted to *General der Nachrichtengruppe* on 1 October 1944 and served as head of signals

Albert Praun entered the Army in October 1913 and served as a platoon leader from January 1915 with the rank of *Leutnant*. He remained in the Army after the war and served as an instructor at the War Academy in Berlin from October 1934. From August 1939 he served as commander of Signals Battalion 38 in Würzburg with the rank of *Major*. From 1940 he served as Signals Officer with various commands, which included Panzer Group Guderian in France and later with the Military Administration in north-east occupied France.

and all communications of the Armed Forces until the end of war. He also served during the Dönitz Government in this capacity until the downfall of the German government on 15 May 1945. He was sent to Cherbourg, where he was interrogated and then transferred to various German prisons. These included Bad Hersfeld, where he remained until June 1947. In 1950 the French government requested his extradition to France to face war crime charges but the US occupation forces denied this, stating there was not enough evidence against him. However, in January 1955 a French court in Marseilles tried Praun in absentia and found him guilty of the murder of nineteen French Resistance members. He was sentenced to death on 1 February 1955 but the sentence was never carried out.

Helmuth Georg HUFENBACH
Generalmajor

* 27 February 1908, Rüstersiel, Wilhelmshaven-Rüsterseil, Hannover
+ 27 March 1945 Kahlholz, East Prussia

Knight's Cross: Awarded on 30 October 1943 as *Oberstleutnant* and Commander of Grenadier Regiment 667, part of the 370th Infantry Division, for his leadership during the defence of the northern sector of the Kuban Bridgehead on the night of 30 September–1 October 1943. His success was mainly due to his critical decision as to when the bulk of the Army corps should cross the heavily armoured sector of the front. Hufenbach was able to master the situation, which allowed his troops and the rest of the division to cross the area and defeat the Soviet forces. On 1 November 1943 he was promoted to the rank of *Oberst* and took part in the retreat through Ukraine. In August and September 1944 the division was encircled and virtually destroyed at Kishinev in Romania. Hufenbach, together with a few surviving members of the division, was able to escape to safety and joined the 15th and 76th Infantry Divisions. Hufenbach attended the 16th Divisional Leaders Course between

Helmuth Hufenbach entered the Army as a volunteer with Infantry Regiment 1 in April 1928 and was commissioned as a *Leutnant* in July 1934. He later served as a Signals Officer and then company commander with Infantry Regiment 24. He later saw action on the Western Front during the invasion of France from May 1940.

November and December 1944, and from 22 January 1945 he took over the leadership of the 562nd *Volksgrenadier* Division.

Knight's Cross with Oakleaves: He became the 807th recipient posthumously on 28 March 1945 as *Oberst* and Leader of the 562nd *Volksgrenadier* Division while attached to the 4th Army and distinguished himself during the heavy fighting in early 1945 near Königsberg. On 28 February he achieved outstanding defensive success in repelling thirty-two Soviet attacks and destroyed thirty enemy tanks during some of the bloodiest battles of the Soviet campaign. On 27 March, during heavy fighting in woods near Kahlholz in East Prussia, Hufenbach was killed and shortly after was posthumously promoted to the rank of *Generalmajor*.

Friedrich Julius Oskar MIETH
General der Infanterie

* 4 June 1888, Eberswalde, Brandenburg
+ 2 September 1944 near Iasi, Romania

Knight's Cross: Awarded on 2 November 1943 as *General der Infanterie* and Commanding General of the IV. Army Corps while attached to the 6th Army for his leadership during the fierce fighting on the Mius Front in August 1943. Mieth had to operate almost blindly as he had received no orders and few reports, receiving no contact with the main body of the 6th Army. Mieth was unaware that the 6th Army were disintegrating but he was a highly capable officer who had previously been a staff officer on the General Staff.

Knight's Cross with Oakleaves: He became the 409th recipient on 1 March 1944 as *General der Infanterie* and Commanding General of the IV. Army Corps for his command during the heavy fighting for the Nikopol Bridgehead during the winter of 1943–44. He took part in the tough defensive battles as part of Army Group South in the Nikopol area, being responsible for creating

Friedrich Mieth entered the Army in 1900, seeing action during the First World War as an *Oberleutnant* while serving on the General Staff of the Army. He remained in the Army after the war, serving in the General Staff once again until February 1930. In October 1935 he served as training officer at the Berlin War Academy with the rank of *Oberst*. From November 1939 he was Chief of the General Staff of the 1st Army and from early 1940 was serving in the Office of the Chief of Operations of the Army with the rank of *Generalleutnant*.

a link with the German troops in the Crimea. He was presented with the Oakleaves by Hitler at *Führer* Headquarters the Wolf's Lair, Rastenburg, in mid-1944. From late August his corps was pushed back across Romania with Mieth ordering a series of desperate attacks against the Soviets, which all failed due to the exhaustion of his troops and the difficult terrain. By the 26th the attacks against his forces were even more severe and he ordered a mass retreat with all carts burned and all unwanted horses shot. Without food or rest the IV. Army Corps began to disintegrate. Mieth tried to break out and ordered his officers to form small battle groups. On 29 August the headquarters of his army corps was overrun by the Soviets and his Chief of Staff *Oberst* Günther Siedschlag was killed. However, Mieth escaped and was up front with his assault unit when it crossed the Berlad River under Soviet artillery fire. On 2 September Mieth was killed during close combat as the Soviets seized the bridge over the Berlad River at Chitani. His corps then ceased to exist.

<u>Max</u> Johannes Heinrich ULICH
Generalmajor

* 25 March 1896, Schönefled, Brandenburg
+ 27 May 1964, Pullach, Munich

Knight's Cross: Awarded on 2 November 1943 as *Oberst* and Commander of the Motorised Grenadier Regiment 15 of the 29th Panzer Grenadier Division for his part in the destruction of ten to twelve tanks near Stalingrad. Shortly after receiving his award he became ill and was transferred to the Reserves until the end of March 1944, when he was appointed Chief of the General Staff of the Commanding General of the Deputy of the VII. Army Corps and Commander of Military District VII in Munich. In December he was promoted to *Generalmajor* and in April 1945 he was appointed commander of the 212th *Volksgrenadier* Division and charged with the defence of Dachau concentration camp. He was instructed by *SS-Gruppenführer* Max Simon to defend the town and Dachau and the camp against approaching American troops. He refused and disobeyed his orders and withdrew his troops, which allowed the camp to be liberated by US troops on 28 April 1945. Ulrich, however, was charged with disobeying orders and court martial proceedings were initiated but he fell ill and was admitted to hospital. While he was there the war ended and as a result all charges were dropped.

Friedrich BLÜMKE
Generalmajor

* 18 February 1898, Rahnwerder, Pomerania
+ 4 September 1944, at a field hospital in Dniester, Soviet Union

Knight's Cross: Awarded on 6 November 1943 as *Oberst* and Commander of Grenadier Regiment 347 as part of the 197th Infantry Division for his part in the prevention of a large-scale enemy breakthrough attempt on the central sector of the Eastern Front, north-east of Orsha. He led his regiment with great skill and despite having been hindered by a battle wound he led his men in a very successful counter-attack, which succeeded in pushing back enemy attacks. A few weeks later he took part in the fighting west of Smolensk and was transferred to the Reserves in January 1944. From 15 March until 20 April Blümke attended the 10th Divisional Leaders Course and from early May was attached to Army Group Ukraine. On 5 July he took over the leadership of the 257th Infantry Division, saw action during the retreat from the Dnieper region and took part in the encirclement near Kishinev. On 24 August Blümke was severely wounded when the vehicle he was travelling in was attacked by enemy aircraft near Tighin. Struck in the chest by a large piece of shrapnel, he was taken to a field hospital in Dniester, where he died. He was posthumously promoted to *Generalmajor* on 20 September 1944.

Friedrich Blümke entered the Army in November 1916, was assigned to Infantry Regiment 42 and was commissioned as a *Leutnant* two years later. He served as a company commander and remained in the Army after the war. He was promoted to *Hauptmann* in May 1933 and transferred into the Reich War Ministry in October 1935. He later served as Chief of Operations with the 23rd Division and was promoted to *Oberstleutnant* in January 1939, seeing action during the invasion of Poland and later in France. From May 1941 he was Acting Chief if the General Staff of the VII. Army Corps and later saw action in the Ukraine and the Soviet Union as Chief of the General Staff of the XIV. Army Corps under the command of *General der Infanterie* Gustav Wietersheim.

<u>Werner</u> Egbert Theodor Martin GOERITZ
Generalleutnant

* 9 March 1892, Braunschweig
\+ 27 May 1958, Bad Tölz, Bavaria

Knight's Cross: Awarded on 6 November 1943 as *Generalleutnant* and Commander of the 291st Infantry Division while attached to the LIX. Army Corps for actions with Army Group South in Kiev, where his command suffered heavy losses. From 10 February 1944 he took command of the 92nd Infantry Division, which was a new division and was sent into action for the first time under the command of Goeritz in May 1944. However, the commander of the 14th Army, *Generaloberst* Eberhard von Mackensen, was far from satisfied with its performance and reported it unfit for combat. As a result it was dissolved in June, just before Goerlitz was wounded and hospitalised, and placed in the *Führer* Reserve until the end of the war. He went into Allied captivity from 1 May 1945 and was released on 28 June that same year.

Werner Goeritz entered the Army in March 1911, serving as adjutant with Infantry Regiment 169 at the start of the First World War. Later he served as 1st Orderly Officer and company leader, and was promoted to *Oberleutnant* in December 1915. He remained in the Army after the war and by 1932 had been promoted to the rank of *Major*. Three years later he was serving with the 17th Division. From October 1936 he was commander of the III. Battalion of Infantry Regiment 35 with the rank of *Oberstleutnant*. From May 1940 he saw action during the invasion of France and was later appointed commander of the *Wehrmacht* Transportation Department in Paris.

Arthur FINGER
Generalmajor

* 18 January 1898, Mocker, West Prussia
\+ 27 January 1945 near Częstochowa, Poland

Knight's Cross: Awarded on 16 November 1943 as *Oberst* and Commander of Artillery Regiment 306 while attached to the 306th Infantry Division for action in Nikopol, Ukraine. He led his regiment until 10 January 1944,

Arthur Finger was a war volunteer from August 1914 with Field Infantry Regiment 81 and later transferred to Reserve Field Artillery Regiment 36. When the war was over he joined the police, where he served for fifteen years, returning to the Army in 1935 with the rank of *Hauptmann*. From September 1939 he was commander of Heavy Artillery Battalion 757. From October the following year he was commander of Artillery Regiment 214, seeing action in Norway, and he was promoted to *Oberst* in February 1942.

when he entered the Reserves and from February he attended the 9th Divisional Leaders Course and was briefly attached to the Army Personnel Office. From 12 April he was attached to Army Group North Ukraine as a temporary divisional commander and from July he was appointed to the leadership of the 291st Infantry Division. He saw action near Lublin and later near the Vistula River. On 1 October Finger was promoted to *Generalmajor* and on 27 January 1945 he was listed as missing in action. It was later confirmed in June 1946 that he had been killed near Częstochowa in Poland when his battle group was attacked by Soviet tanks.

Kurt RÖPKE
General der Infanterie

* 29 November 1896, Solingen, Rhine Province
+ 21 July 1966, Göttingen, Lower Saxony

Knight's Cross: Awarded on 17 November 1943 as *Generalmajor* and Commander of the 46th Infantry Division as part of the XXXX. Panzer Corps for his outstanding leadership on the Russian Front. His exploits were described in the press on 1 November 1943, 'The Knight's Cross was awarded to Generalmajor Röpke the Commander of an infantry division who personally took responsibility of two enemy penetrations south of Dnepropetrovsk and eliminated them by leading various counter-attacks.' He later led his command in the retreat through the southern Ukraine, where it once again took heavy casualties. Röpke was promoted to *Generalleutnant* in February 1944 and continued to command his division, seeing action during the withdrawal through Transylvania, until

July. From 12 September Röpke took over as temporary commander of the XXIX. Army Corps, seeing action in southern Ukraine, where in December he was promoted to *General der Infanterie.*

Knight's Cross with Oakleaves: He became the 830th recipient on 14 April 1945 as *General der Infanterie* and Commanding General of the XXIX. Army Corps while attached to the 8th Army for his leadership during the battles in Upper Hungary, where he led with distinction during the fighting in the Carpathians. He saw further action during the retreat to northern Hungary and into Slovakia, and was wounded on 8 May 1945 near Pisek in Czechoslovakia. He surrendered his command to US troops at the same time and was handed over to the Soviets on 20 May 1945. Röpke was imprisoned in various NKVD prison camps, before being tried by a Military Tribunal in Kiev for so-called war crimes. He was sentenced to twenty-five years' forced labour on 30 October 1947 but was repatriated on 7 January 1956 thanks to a general amnesty.

Kurt Röpke joined the 7th Company of Infantry Regiment 57 in April 1914 and was commissioned as a *Leutnant* seven months later. He saw action during the First World War as an adjutant, company leader and deputy battalion leader, and remained in the Army after the war. He was attached to the Infantry School in Döberitz from October 1935 and later served as an instructor. From August 1940, now with the rank of *Oberstleutnant*, he served as Commander of Infantry Regiment 50, seeing action during the French campaign.

Maximilian Albert FELZMANN
General der Artillerie

* 22 April 1894, Zwittau, Czechoslovakia
+ 8 June 1962, Zürich, Switzerland

Knight's Cross: Awarded on 28 November 1943 as *Generalmajor* and Commander of the 251st Infantry Division for his part in the prevention of a Soviet breakthrough around the Dnieper area despite his command having been reduced to the strength of just 5,000 men. At the beginning of December, Felzmann was promoted to *Generalleutnant* and took over as commander of Corps Detachment E, a command formed by the remnants of both the 137th and 36th Infantry Divisions, which he led with great success during the summer of 1944.

Knight's Cross with Oakleaves: Awarded on 3 November 1944 as the 643rd recipient as *Generalleutnant* and Commander of Corps Battalion E for his bitter defence during the breakout of Brest-Litvosk. He defended the city with his troops for three days against two Soviet armies, and on 27 July he led his troops out of the city, saving at least 75 per cent of his command. Felzmann was promoted to *General der Artillerie* on 1 January 1945 and was personally presented with the Oakleaves by the Commander-in-Chief of Army Group North *Generaloberst* Walter Weiss a few days later. He was at this time appointed Commanding General of the XXVII. Army Corps, seeing action in Western Prussia until mid-April, when he took over as the Commanding General of the Replacement V. Army Corps and Commander in Military

General der Artillerie and Commanding General of the XXVII. Army Corps Maximilian Felzmann is seen here with *Hauptmann* Josef Brandner, commander of Army Assault Artillery Brigade 912, after presenting him with the Knight's Cross in March 1945.

District V, Stuttgart. On 8 May 1945 he surrendered to American troops and remained in Allied custody until his release on 25 June 1947.

Dr Hermann HOHN
Generalleutnant

* 11 October 1897, Renchen, Baden
+ 13 November 1968, Ladenburg, Baden-Württemberg

Knight's Cross: Awarded on 28 November 1943 as *Oberst* and *Führer* of the 72nd Infantry Division as part of the III. Army Corps for actions in the Soviet Union. From 14 November his division was stationed as the primary defender of the city of Cherkassy on the Dnieper Front against a much superior enemy. The following day Hohn launched an attack against the Soviet bridgehead, which paid off, and by doing so prevented the Soviet forces from penetrating the front lines of the Germans. On 22 November the Soviets launched an artillery assault and managed to create a broad gap in the German front line and penetrate their rear defences. Together with the simultaneous assault east of Cherkassy, there was a real danger that the city would be encircled by the Soviets. Hohn made the independent decision to send in a battle group from the south into the rear of the enemy, which played a major role in the Soviet force being destroyed south-east of Cherkassy.

Knight's Cross with Oakleaves: He became the 410th recipient on 1 March 1944 as *Oberst* and Commander of the 72nd Infantry Division as part of the XXXXII. Army Corps for continued actions near Cherkassy in the Soviet Union. Hohn became the soul of the resistance of his division. He repeatedly reorganised the defences on his own initiative and in doing so prevented the enemy's sought-after breakthrough.

Hermann Hohn entered the Army in January 1915, served with Artillery Regiment 10 until May 1916 and was commissioned as a *Leutnant* the following year. He retired from Army service in December 1920 and studied Political Economics at University in Heidelberg, later working as an accountant at a local bank. He re-joined the Army in October 1935 and saw action during the Second World War as adjutant of the 72nd Infantry Division from November 1939.

Hohn was presented with the Oakleaves by Hitler in May 1944 at the Berghof on the Obersalzburg and he had by that time been promoted to *Generalmajor*. In July he was appointed commander of the 72nd Infantry Division, which had been re-formed in Poland in the summer months, and was officially cited for its performance in the Vistula defensive battles in August.

Knight's Cross with Oakleaves and Swords: Awarded on 31 October 1944 as the 109th recipient as *Generalmajor* and Commander of the 72nd Infantry Division while still attached to the XXXXII. Army Corps for his outstanding leadership of his division during the fighting in the summer of 1944 in the Ostrówek area of the Eastern Front, where it suffered heavy casualties. The award was personally presented to Hohn by Hitler sometime in December 1944 at Führer Headquarters Alderhorst in Bad Nauheim. On 12 January 1945 his command suffered heavy casualties once again in southern Poland and was smashed in the Battle of the Baranov Bridgehead. On 30 January Hohn was promoted to *Generalleutnant* and from April he was given the leadership of the XI. Army Corps and saw heavy fighting on the Eastern Front until 9 May 1945, when he surrendered his command to the Allies.

Martin Siegfried Harald GAREIS
General der Infanterie

* 6 October 1891, Berlin-Niederbarnim, Brandenburg
+ 26 February 1976, Kreuth, Bavaria

Knight's Cross: Awarded on 29 November 1943 as *Generalleutnant* and Commander of the 98th Infantry Division while attached to the XXXIX. Army Corps for actions during heavy fighting in the Crimea, where he distinguished himself and was mentioned by name in the Wehrmacht communiqué of 16 November 1943. In May 1944 he took over command of the 264th Infantry Division in Croatia and then in October he entered the Reserves until January 1945, when he took over the leadership of the XXXXVI. Panzer Corps. He saw action in Warsaw as part of the 9th Army and from March he led his Panzer Corps in West Prussia, now as part of the 2nd Army. He was promoted to *General der Artillerie* on 1 April and continued to command his panzer corps until he surrendered his command on 2 May 1945 to British forces. From 8 May until mid-June 1945 Gareis served as liaison officer between the headquarters of British Field Marshal Montgomery and the British Army prisoner of war camps. He was released from British captivity in June 1947.

Martin Gareis entered the Army Cadet Corps in December 1909 and attended the War School in Potsdam. He saw action during the First World War and was wounded in October 1914, later serving as a *Leutnant* and company leader with Infantry Regiment 24. He later served as an orderly officer and regimental adjutant, remaining in the Army after the war. By October 1935 he held the rank of *Major* and was battalion commander with Infantry Regiment 2. In 1939 Gareis commanded Infantry Regiment 282, seeing action during the invasion of France from May 1940.

<u>Erich</u> Otto Ludwig BUSCHENHAGEN
General der Infanterie

* 8 December 1895, Straßburg, Alsace
+ 13 September 1994, Kronberg, Hesse

Knight's Cross: Awarded on 5 December 1943 as *Generalleutnant* and Commander of the 15th Infantry Division of the LII. Army Corps for actions during the Soviet breakthrough on 15 October 1943 near Piatykhatky, where his forces stabilised the front in the sector north of Krivoi Rog. Buschenhagen saw action on the Eastern Front from mid-1942, taking part in the fighting at Kharkov and in the Donets area. His command suffered heavy losses at the Battle of Dnepropetrovsk in the summer of 1943. He then took over command of the LII. Army Corps from late 1943 but in early January 1944 the Russians pushed back his corps and Kirovograd was taken. Promoted to *General der Infanterie* in February, his command was later deployed to north-west of Odessa as part of the 8th Army and later retreated behind the Dniester until May 1944.

Erich Buschenhagen entered the Army in March 1914, was attached to the 16th Reserve Division and was commissioned as a *Leutnant* the following year. He was assigned to the XXX. Reserve Corps until October 1916 and then served as adjutant of Army Radio Commander 1, ending the war as German Liaison Officer of the Chief of Signals. He stayed in the Army after the war and from October 1936 he was commander of Signals Troop III. At the start of the Second World War he was serving as an *Oberst* and Chief of the General Staff of the XXI. Army Corps.

Knight's Cross with Oakleaves: He became the 521st recipient on 4 July 1944 as *General der Infanterie* and Commanding General of the LII. Army Corps while attached to the 6th Army for smashing the Soviet bridgeheads on the lower Dniester. He was personally presented with the Oakleaves by Hitler in July 1944 at *Führer* headquarters, the Wolf's Lair, East Prussia. In late August he saw heavy action against the Soviets near the Pruth River, where the remnants of the XXX., XXXXIV. and his LII. Army Corps had gathered on an island that was being pulverised by Soviet artillery. In a breakout attempt made on the evening of 28 August led by officers and about 10,000 to 12,000 soldiers, some drowned, while others collapsed from exhaustion and a great many were killed. Buschenhagen and a small band of his men managed to evade the encirclement and head for the Carpathians on foot. However, in early September most of his men were captured by Soviet troops. In June 1950 Buschenhagen was sentenced to twenty-five years imprisonment by a Soviet court but he was released in October 1955 on a general amnesty.

Hermann Emil FLÖRKE
Generalleutnant

* 23 October 1893, Hannover, Lower Saxony
+ 19 August 1979, Gießen, Hesse

Knight's Cross: Awarded on 15 December 1943 as *Generalmajor* and Commander of the 14th Infantry Division, part of the VI. Army Corps, for actions during the fighting around Vitebsk in the Soviet Union. He succeeded in halting a major Soviet offensive that had begun on 8 November and he launched an attack against the front east of the city and stopped the Soviets in their tracks. Flörke continued to lead the division with great success during the fighting in Vitebsk and it was almost ripped apart in July 1944 and escaped total destruction, but was later reduced to battle group strength.

Knight's Cross with Oakleaves: He became the 565th recipient on 2 September 1944 as *Generalleutnant* and Commander of the 14th Infantry Division while attached to the 2nd Army for his distinguished service and bravery during the desperate battles on the Soviet Front near Grodno in Belarus, Osowiec and Łomża in Poland. The Oakleaves were personally presented to Flörke by Hitler sometime in early November 1944 at *Führer*

Hermann Flörke entered the Army in September 1914, serving with Infantry Regiment 74 with the rank of *Leutnant*. He remained in the Army after the First World War and was attached to Infantry Regiment 12, and then from 1935 he was attached to the Inspector of War Schools. From March 1939 Flörke was battalion commander with Infantry Regiment 53 with the rank of *Oberstleutnant*. In February 1940 he took over as commander of Infantry Regiment 53, seeing action in France.

Headquarters, the Wolf's Lair in Rastenburg. From 18 February 1945 he took the leadership of the LXVI. Army Corps, seeing action in the Eifel mountain area of Germany and in the Ruhr district as part of Army Group D. Flörke was captured by US forces on 21 April and remained in Allied captivity until 1 June 1947.

Erpo Bodo Wilke Kraft von BODENHAUSEN
Generalleutnant

* 12 April 1897, Arnstein, Witzenhausen
+ 9 May 1945 near Grobiņa in Liepāja, Latvia

Knight's Cross: Awarded on 17 December 1943 as *Generalleutnant* and Commander of the 12th Panzer Division, part of the 2nd Army, for actions near the defensive front by the Netech River in Kalinkawitschy in south-eastern Belarus. In January 1944, as part of Army Group North, his division was sent to help with the breaking of the Siege of Leningrad but arrived too late. He later distinguished himself during the retreat across the Baltic State. Later in the summer of 1944, Army Group North tried to prevent the encirclement of the 4th and 9th Armies and Bodenhausen, where his division took part, but it failed and the Soviets pushed them into the Courland Pocket. From 12 April he was delegated with the leadership of the L. Army Corps while still fighting in the Courland area. On 9 May 1945 he committed suicide near Grobiņa, Liepāja, in Latvia, rather than be taken prisoner by the Soviets.

Erpo Freiherr von Bodenhausen entered the Army in October 1914 and fought with Dragoon Regiment 5 during the First World War. He was commissioned as a *Leutnant* in July 1915 and awarded both classes of the Iron Cross while serving as a platoon leader. He remained in the Army after the war, serving with Cavalry Regiment 11 and Mounted Regiment 16, and was promoted to *Oberleutnant* in July 1925. From March 1931 he was attached to the Staff of the 3rd Cavalry Division and in 1933 served as Chief of the Training Squadron of Mounted Regiment 13. From June 1936 he was adjutant of the 12th Division with the rank of *Major* and at the beginning of the war he served as *Oberstleutnant* and Commander of the II. Battalion of Cavalry Rifle Regiment 8.

Ernst MEINERS
Generalmajor der Reserve

* 13 June 1893, Berlin
+ 11 June 1959, Stuttgart

Knight's Cross: Awarded on 17 December 1943 as *Oberst der Reserve* and Commander of Grenadier Regiment 161 of the 81st Infantry Division for actions during the assault against Hill 204 in the Soviet Union. This assault will be forever remembered as one of the hardest days for his regiment against an enemy that dominated an important railway line along two major supply routes. For two days the German counter-attacks had failed, however Meiners developed an attack plan of his own and mounted a major assault on Hill 204. The attack was over in less than an hour and the enemy was smashed. It was such an achievement that his entire regiment was overjoyed and Hitler awarded Meiners the Knight's Cross. From mid-May 1944 he was appointed deputy commander of the 263rd Infantry Division, seeing action in the Baltic States, and from June he served in a similar capacity with the 290th Infantry Division in the same area. From 15 July he was sent to Stuttgart, where he formed the 547th Grenadier Division and was promoted to *Generalmajor der Reserve* in October when his command of the division was confirmed. He took part in the retreat through Poland, and in the battles of East Prussia. His division was pushed back to the Danzig area, where from October it was redesignated a *Volksgrenadier* Division. On 8 February 1945 Meiners was wounded near Zinten in East Prussia and removed from the front, replaced by *Generalmajor* Erich Fronhöfer. He entered the Reserves and was attached to area command in Breslau and later captured by US troops in Pisek, Czechoslovakia, on 9 May 1945. He was handed over to the Soviets and was sentenced to twenty-five years' hard labour by a Military Tribunal in Moscow. He was finally released on a general amnesty and returned to Germany on 11 October 1955.

Friedrich Maximilian Heinrich SIXT
Generalleutnant

* 28 October 1895, Munich, Bavaria
+ 4 August 1976, Icking, Bavaria

Knight's Cross: Awarded on 17 December 1943 as *Generalleutnant* and Commander of the 50th Infantry Division while attached to the XXXXIX. Mountain Corps for actions on the Russian Front. On 1 November 1943 Sixt, together with his divisional staff, were ordered to form Group Sixt and take control of the defence of the Perekop Isthmus. This was a narrow piece of land that connected the Crimean Peninsula to the mainland of Ukraine and it was Sixt who became responsible for preventing a Soviet breakthrough into the Crimea – which he succeeded in doing. In May 1944, during the fierce fighting in the Crimea, the 50th Infantry Division was almost destroyed. On the night of 11 May he was one of the last troops to be evacuated to the mainland by the German Navy. By August that year he had recovered enough to return to the Eastern Front as commander of the 5th *Jäger* Division.

Knight's Cross with Oakleaves: He became the 772nd recipient on 11 March 1945 as *Generalleutnant* and Commander of the 5th *Jäger* Division as part of the XXIII. Army Corps for his part in the defensive battles along the Bug and Narew Rivers in autumn 1944. At the beginning of the offensive he took control of many critical situations and in particular a strong Soviet flank attack that came at a time when his division was already heavily engaged with the enemy. However, with a handful of assault gun battalions, he was able to push back the Soviet attack while leading from the front. It was down to his excellent leadership that the division was able to retreat towards the Vistula and he had the distinction of his being the only formation of the 2nd Army originally positioned along the Narew to reach the west side of the Vistula with all its artillery and supply troops. From mid-April 1945 he took command of the CI. Army Corps and was able to advance towards the western allies near the Elbe, surrendering to British troops on 8 May 1945.

Johannes 'Hans' BRUHN
Generalmajor

* 10 July 1898, Nemünster, Schleswig-Holstein
+ 20 November 1955, Lübeck, Schleswig-Holstein

Knight's Cross: Awarded on 20 December 1943 as *Oberst* and Artillery Commander 149 for actions during the clearance operation at the Kuban Bridgehead area as part of the V. Army Corps. From April 1944 the Soviets advanced across the Kerch Strait, which meant the Crimean Peninsula could no longer be held and resulted in his command having to retreat towards Sevastopol. In May the German defence fell and his command was evacuated across the Black Sea, upon which he joined the Staff of the XI. SS Army Corps. In September Bruhn attended the 14th Divisional Leaders Course and from the 30th he took the leadership of the 553rd Volksgrenadier Division. From 1 November, with his promotion to *Generalmajor*, he was confirmed as divisional Commander. He saw action on the Western Front from mid-November, where he took part in the defence of the Saverne Gap in the Vosges Mountain region against the US 7th Army. On 22 November Bruhn and his staff were captured by French and British troops and held as prisoners until June 1947. In 1951 he briefly joined the German Federal Border Guards, also known as the Federal Police, but retired just three years later due to ill health.

Johannes 'Hans' Bruhn entered Army service with Field Artillery Regiment 9 in June 1915 as a war volunteer, being commissioned as a *Leutnant* in June 1918. In April 1920 he joined the Protection Police in Berlin and remained there until April 1935, when he transferred back into the Army with the rank of *Major*. He attended various courses and from October 1937 was battalion commander with Artillery Regiment 39, in August 1939 becoming commander with Heavy Artillery Battalion 602. From December 1940 he served with the Chief of the Army Armaments and Commander of the Replacement Army with the rank of *Oberstleutnant*.

Gottfried FRÖLICH
Generalmajor

* 3 June 1894, Dresden, Saxony
\+ 30 July 1959, Heidenheim an der Brenz, Baden-Württemberg

Knight's Cross: Awarded on 20 December 1943 as *Oberst* and *Führer* of the 8th Panzer Division of the XIII. Army Corps for defensive actions near Lipówka on the Soviet Front. During a particularly heavy mortar attack Frölich rushed forward towards retreating soldiers, halted them and reorganised them and set up renewed defensive positions. It was his fearless personal attitude and bravery that reversed this dangerous crisis and created a new defensive line along the Makaroff and Korolowka road, which was held against all enemy attacks. However, during the next few hours enemy pressure against Frölich's division intensified and he realised that if the enemy succeeded in tying down or pushing back the 8th Panzer Division it would create a danger to the German corps that were approaching. Frölich could not wait for orders as all communication links to his command had been destroyed and therefore he took the decision to block the way to the Kiev–Zhitomir road with his division. He ordered his men to retreat from the enemy and establish a new defensive line and later he received similar orders to what he had done himself and the commanding general would eventually agree with Frölich's decision. The personal example set by Frölich inspired his soldiers throughout

Gottfried Frölich entered the Army with the II. Replacement Battalion of Field Artillery Regiment 48 in August 1914, and was wounded at the front in May 1916. In July he returned to action and was commissioned as a *Leutnant*, remaining in the Army after the war and being appointed battalion commander with Artillery Regiment 14 from October 1935 with the rank of *Major*. He later attended the Artillery School in Jüterbog and from October 1939 served as commander of Artillery Regiment 78 during the invasion of France.

the heavy fighting and they were able to ward off all enemy attacks for the entire day, preventing more enemy attacks. Rarely has a Knight's Cross been more deserved. As a result of his bravery and leadership he was promoted to the rank of *Generalmajor* three weeks before he was informed of his award. In April 1944 Frölich was ill and admitted to hospital, returning to his panzer division on 20 July and seeing action in northern Ukraine, southern Poland and in Slovakia before being admitted to hospital once again on 22 January 1945. From 18 March until the beginning of April he was leader of Corps Group *von Tettau*, an ad hoc unit formed mainly of *Volkssturm* (the German equivalent of the Home Guard) and training units to defend two key cities along the Baltic coast. In April he was named as the Higher Artillery Commander of the 3rd Panzer Army and in early May he surrendered to British troops.

Richard JOHN
Generalleutnant

* 21 June 1896, Wilhelmshaven, Hannover
+ 20 February 1965, Garmisch-Partenkirchen, Bavaria

Knight's Cross: Awarded on 20 December 1943 as *Generalmajor* and Commander of the 292nd Infantry Division of the XXXV. Army Corps for his bravery and leadership during the fierce fighting in Gomel against the Soviets. The Germans had occupied the city from August 1941 and by the end of November 1943 the city was back in the hands of the Soviet Union again but at a price – nearly 80 per cent of it had been destroyed. He later took part in the fighting on the Sozh and the Pripyat marshes in Ukraine during Operation Bagration, the code name of the strategic operation against Soviet forces by Army Group Centre. John was promoted to *Generalleutnant* in April 1944 and in July he was appointed Head of the Department for Ballistics and Munitions in the Army Weapons Office. From November he took over as Chief of the Office Group for the Development and Testing, where he remained until the end of the war.

Richard John entered the Army in August 1914 with Bavarian Infantry Regiment 1 and was commissioned as a *Leutnant* in May 1915. He later served as a platoon leader and was wounded in July 1918, ending the war as a company leader. He remained in the Army and from October 1936 served as Operations Officer in the Army Weapons Office with the rank of *Major*. From January 1940 he served as battalion commander with Infantry Regiment 203 and was promoted to *Oberst* in October when he was appointed commander of Infantry Regiment 36 during occupation duty in France.

Erich Hans Christian Dietrich DETHLEFFSEN
Generalmajor

* 2 August 1904, Kiel
+ 4 July 1980, Munich, Bavaria

Knight's Cross: Awarded on 23 December 1943 as *Oberst im Generalstab* and Chief of the General Staff of the XXXIX. Panzer Corps for actions during the defence of Smolensk on the Russian Front. From the beginning of 1944 he saw action in the Orsha area as part of the 4th Army and in May the Panzer Corps withdrew to an area east of Mogilev. He remained on the Eastern Front when on 5 May he was appointed Chief of the General Staff of the 4th Army under the command of *Generaloberst* Gotthard Heinrici. He was promoted to *Generalmajor* in November 1944 and from February 1945 he was admitted to the Reserve Hospital in Detmold, where an old injury he had received earlier in the war was causing problems once again. From 15 March 1945 he was given the brief leadership of Division Group *Raegener*, and from 23 March he was appointed Chief of the Operations Group with the *Wehrmacht* Operations Staff. He held this appointment after Hitler's death and served in this capacity throughout the Dönitz Government until 23 May 1945, when he was arrested by the British. He was transferred to the US prison camp known as Camp Ashcan in Mondorf-les-Bains in Luxembourg. For a time he was held with former Foreign Minister Joachim von Ribbentrop and *Reichsmarschall* Hermann Göring until his release on 31 March 1948.

Erich Dethleffsen entered the Army in November 1923 with Infantry Regiment 8 and attended various courses before being commissioned as a *Leutnant* in 1927. He was promoted to *Oberleutnant* in January 1931 and served as adjutant with Infantry Regiment 1, later being attached to the War Academy. From April 1939 he was attached to the Army General Staff with the rank of *Hauptmann*.

Ralph Georg Edgar Joachim Eddo Lobo da Silveira Graf von ORIOLA
Generalleutnant

* 9 August 1895, Herischdorf-Hirschberg, Schleswig
+ 28 April 1970, Freiburg im Breisen, Württemberg

Knight's Cross: Awarded on 23 December 1943 as *Generalleutnant* and Commander of the 299th Infantry Division of the XXXV. Army Corps for actions during the Battles of Bryansk and Gomel in the Soviet Union. Not only did Oriola distinguish himself in battle but the entire division was praised by the Army High Command. However, three of its infantry battalions had to be disbanded due to heavy casualties and the 299th Infantry Division was rested. On 22 June 1944 the Soviets launched a massive summer offensive with 2.5 million men. Their opening attack struck Oriola's 299th Infantry Division and it collapsed within a few hours. Only remnants escaped, and *Generalleutnant* Oriola was one of the lucky ones and served on the staff of the VI. Army Corps until August 1944. In January 1945 he took over as temporary commander of the VI. Army Corps and form mid-February he took over as commander of the XIII. Army Corps and saw action in the Battle of East Pomerania. He ended the war fighting in West Prussia and was captured by British troops on 31 March 1945. He was kept in Allied captivity until 17 May 1948.

Guido Ernst Alfred Konstantin Mortimer von KESSEL
General der Panzertruppe

* 25 May 1893, Arnswalde, Germany
+ 8 January 1981, Goslar, Germany

Knight's Cross: Awarded on 28 December 1943 as *Generalmajor* and Commander of the 20th Panzer Division while attached to the 9th Army for his leadership and bravery during the summer offensive in Kursk. He made a counter-attack in the area around Vitebsk against two Soviet companies, which were smashed and his troops captured twelve heavy machine guns and nine anti-tank rifles. Shortly before he was presented with the award he was promoted to *Generalleutnant* and took part in many battles on the Eastern Front.

Knight's Cross with Oakleaves: He became the 611th recipient on 16 October 1944 as *Generalleutnant* and Commander of the 20th Panzer Division as part of

Mortimer von Kessel entered the Army in August 1914 as a war volunteer with Hussar Regiment 12 and was commissioned as a *Leutnant* in March 1915. He later served as adjutant of his Regiment and was awarded both classes of the Iron Cross during the First World War. He remained in the Army after the war and from October 1935 served as Chief Personnel Officer on the Staff of the 1st Panzer Division with the rank of *Major*. He saw action during the Polish campaign as part of the 3rd Light Division and from November 1939 he served as Department Head in the Army Personnel office.

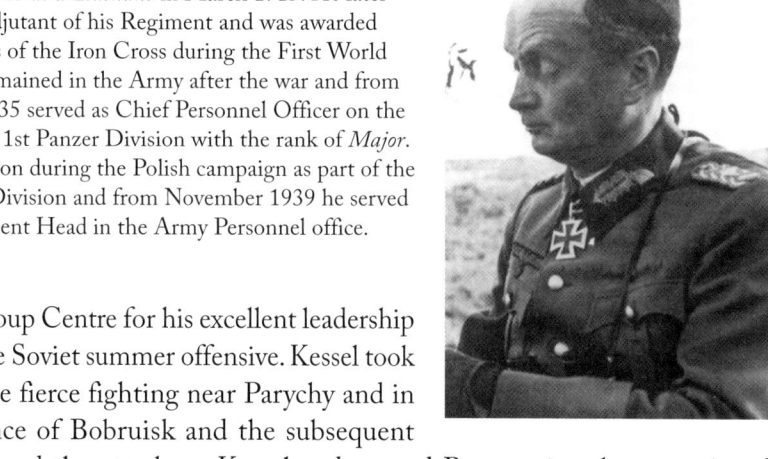

Army Group Centre for his excellent leadership during the Soviet summer offensive. Kessel took part in the fierce fighting near Parychy and in the defence of Bobruisk and the subsequent breakout and the attack on Kessel and around Baranowicze between 1 and 6 June. Later, in the area around Bobruisk, he took part in operations to halt the Soviet strategic offensive, Operation Bagration, from late June to August 1944. It happened at the same time as Operation Overlord in the west, which caused Germany to fight on two major fronts at the same time. By the end of the conflict the Soviets had destroyed twenty-eight of the thirty-four German divisions of Army Group Centre, completely shattering the German front line. It was the largest defeat in German military history, with almost 450,000 German casualties and another 300,000 cut off from the Courland Pocket. On 27 December Kessel was appointed Commanding General of the VII. Panzer Corps and was promoted to *General der Panzertruppe* in March 1945. In the spring he saw action in West Prussia and fought in the final battle in Gdansk, Poland, where shortly after he surrendered to US troops and was held in captivity until 5 June 1947.

August Ludwig <u>Martin</u> BERG
Generalmajor

* 4 April 1905, Arensberg, Saxony-Anhalt
+ 2 April 1969, Kampen, Sylt, Northern Germany

Knight's Cross: Awarded on 30 December 1943 as *Oberst* and Commander of Grenadier Regiment 166 while attached to the 82nd Infantry Division for his distinguished leadership during the latter half of 1943, particularly during the defensive battles near Ssumy and in the retreat to the Dnieper River. In

Martin Berg entered the Police Service in April 1924. A year later he was assigned to the 2nd Protection Police Inspectorate in Berlin and in July was promoted to *Polizei-Wachtmeister*. After attending various courses, he was commissioned as a *Polizei-Leutnant* in August 1927, and in less than two years he was adjutant to the Inspector of Düsseldorf and was promoted to *Polizei-Oberleutnant* in December. From January 1930 he served as Company Officer and later became Course Director at the Police School for Physical Training. From 5 November 1933 he was adjutant to the Commandant of Papenburg Concentration Camp, *SS-Standartenführer* Hans Löritz. From late May 1940 he led the II. Battalion and was awarded the Iron Cross 1st Class on 28 June 1940 for his part in the victory in France and Belgium.

May 1944 he was appointed Commander of the 1st *Skijäger* Infantry Brigade, which from June was at divisional strength. Berg continued to see action on the Eastern Front as part of the 4th Panzer Army and he was promoted to *Generalmajor* in August. On 13 October he was appointed Commander of the 201st Security Division, and then just seven days later he was transferred to the 207th Security Division in the Soviet Union. In November the division was disbanded and together with remnants of a number of regiments, Berg formed the 207th Special Purpose Division Staff. It performed security and rear area tasks until the end of the war. Berg surrendered his command to British forces near Osten in Lower Saxony on 9 May 1945, and he was released in April 1947.

Albert HENZE
Generalleutnant

* 7 August 1894, Kirchhain, Hesse
* 31 March 1979, Ingolstadt, Bavaria

Knight's Cross: Awarded on 15 January 1944 as *Oberst* and Commander of Panzer Grenadier Regiment 110 of the 11th Panzer Division for his distinguished service during operations on the Russian Front between November and December 1943. He took part in the fierce fighting near Cherkassy and later near Berezivka, Novoalexandrovka and Myronivka, where he distinguished himself repeatedly, showing his excellent leadership skills and his gallantry in battle. From 13 February until 3 April 1944 he was appointed Acting Commander of

Panzer Grenadier Division *Feldherrnhalle* and from early May he attended the 11th Divisional Leaders Course, then from July was given the leadership of the 19th *Luftwaffe* Field Division. From August he took over as leader of the 21st *Luftwaffe* Field Division and was promoted to *Generalmajor* on 9 November, when he was confirmed as divisional commander.

Knight's Cross with Oakleaves: He became the 709th recipient on 21 January 1945 as *Generalmajor* and Commander of Group *Henze* with the *Luftwaffe* 21st *Luftwaffe* Field Division as part of the XVI. Army Corps during the heavy fighting in the Courland area. On 24 December 1944 the Soviet forces attacked with six rifle divisions and a tank corps. Henze recognised the danger of a breakthrough and ordered a counter-attack into the flank of the enemy forces. The attack was a great success, with a new defensive line formed where his troops destroyed or damaged ninety Soviet tanks, three assault guns and five artillery guns. On 30 January Henze was appointed Commander of the 30th Infantry Division and took part in the retreat through the Baltic and in six battles of the Courland Pocket. He was promoted to

Albert Henze entered the Army as a war volunteer in August 1914 and was attached to Infantry Regiment 75, being commissioned as a *Leutnant* two years later. When the war was over he briefly served with the Police and returned to the Army in October 1934 as a *Hauptmann*. From August 1939 he served as battalion leader with Infantry Regiment 63 with the rank of *Major* and saw action during the invasion of Poland, later taking part in the French campaign with the 27th Infantry Division.

Generalleutnant on 1 May 1945 and surrendered to Soviet troops just seven days later, remaining imprisoned for the next ten years.

Wilhelm-Francis 'Willifrank' OCHSNER
Generalleutnant

* 31 March 1898, Munich, Bavaria
+ 5 December 1990, Marquartstein, Bavaria

Knight's Cross: Awarded on 18 January 1944 as *Oberst* and Commander of the 31st Infantry Division of the LV. Army Corps for actions on the Russian Front. Ochsner was promoted to *Generalmajor*, led his infantry division during

Wiilhelm Ochsner volunteered to join the Army in September 1915, served with Royal Bavarian Infantry Regiment 1 and was commissioned as a *Leutnant* in June 1916. He remained with the same command throughout most of the war, suffering from nervous exhaustion in April 1918 and being captured by French troops just before the end of the conflict. He stayed in the Army after the war and in January 1938 was appointed Chief of Operations of the 36th Infantry Division with the rank of *Major*. From October 1939 he was Chief of Operations of the VII. Army Corps and saw action during the French campaign.

the Battle of Kursk in July 1943 and later that year took part in the battles of the middle Dnieper and during the retreats through the Soviet Union. In June 1944, now with the rank of *Generalleutnant*, Ochsner and his command, now down in strength, faced the mighty Soviet summer offensive as part of the 4th Army and was by mid-June virtually destroyed. On 30 June Ochnser was taken prisoner by Soviet forces, was later charged with war crimes by a Soviet Military Tribunal in Bobruisk and sentenced in November 1947 to twenty-five years' imprisonment. He was subsequently released together with many other prisoners due to a general amnesty in October 1955.

Rudolf PESCHEL
Generalleutnant

* 21 April 1894, Strassburg, Alsace
+ 30 June 1944 near Vitebsk, Belorussia

Knight's Cross: Awarded on 20 January 1944 as *Generalleutnant* and Commander of the 6th *Luftwaffe* Field Division of the LIII. Army Corps for actions in the Vitebsk area in the central section of the Eastern Front. During the winter of 1943–44 the Soviets made four attempts to take Orsha but were defeated every time. It was Peschel and his field division that especially distinguished itself during these battles, as his command knocked out forty-seven Soviet tanks north-east of Vitebsk, Belorussia, during January 1944. However, in late June his command was surrounded by Soviet forces near Vitebsk together with the 4th *Luftwaffe* Field Division, whose commander, *Generalleutnant* Robert Pistorius, was killed on 27 June. Just three days later, on the morning of the 30th, Peschel was killed during heavy fighting in the same area.

Rudolf Peschel entered the Army in March 1914, served mainly with Infantry Regiment 20 and was commissioned as a *Leutnant* later that year. He then served as a battalion adjutant and company leader and stayed with the Army after the war, rising to the rank of *Oberstleutnant* in August 1937. From December 1939 he served as commander of Infantry Regiment 163, seeing action in France and later in the Soviet Union.

Rudolf STEGMANN
Generalleutnant

* 6 August 1894, Nikolaiken, East Prussia
+ 18 June 1944, Bricquebec-en-Cotentin, Cherbourg, France

Knight's Cross: Awarded on 20 January 1944 as *Generalmajor* and Commander of the 36th Infantry Division while attached to the 9th Army for his excellent leadership and bravery for actions in the Soviet Union. From 10 January Stegmann was assigned to the Reserves to rest and on 1 May 1944 he was appointed commander of the 77th Infantry Division in the Caen area of France.

With the invasion of France by the Allies on 6 June his division was engaged in heavy fighting and was given orders to defend Cherbourg to the last man. However, Stegmann felt it would be an unnecessary sacrifice and so he sent his troops and their valuable equipment to the south and stopped several battalions from moving into the battle zone. On 18 June Stegmann's staff car was attacked by an American fighter-bomber and all the occupants were killed. Stegmann had been recommended for promotion and on 3 July 1944 the elevation to *Generalleutnant* was approved and backdated to 1 June 1944.

Emil Wilhelm VOGEL
General der Gebirgstruppe

* 20 July 1894, Zwickau
+ 1 October 1985, Mülheim

Knight's Cross: Awarded on 7 August 1943 as *Generalleutnant* and Commander of the 101st *Jäger* Division, part of the XXXXIX. Mountain Army Corps, for actions during the invasion of the Soviet Union. Specifically, this was for his leadership during the heavy fighting near Tuapse on the Black Sea in October 1942 and for the crushing of a Soviet bridgehead on 29 and 30 April 1943. It was also awarded for his recapturing the divisions sector on Hill 121 and successfully holding it against strong enemy forces supported by tanks and aircraft in May 1943.

Knight's Cross with Oakleaves: He became the 475th recipient on 14 May 1944 as *Generalleutnant* and Commander of the 101st *Jäger*

Emil Vogel, right, standing with *Generaloberst* Richard Ruoff, Commander-in-Chief of the 17th Army. Vogel entered the Army in April 1905, seeing action during the First World War and being commissioned in June 1915. He remained with the Army after the war and had reached the rank of *Oberstleutnant* by August 1937 and was serving as Operations Officer on the General Staff of the VII. Army Corps. He saw action in Poland from September 1939 and from October 1940 served as Chief of Staff of the XX. Army Corps.

Division as part of the 17th Army for the role his division played during the Kamianets-Podilskyi Pocket battle in western Ukraine. There his division was one of the German units encircled and during the battle his unit formed the rearguard of the LVI. Panzer Corps and he was mentioned in the Armed Forces Report of 29 March 1944 for his performance and leadership. He was presented with the Oakleaves personally by Hitler during a ceremony at the Berghof on the Obersalzburg on 31 May 1944. From 10 August until the end of the war he was the commanding general of the XXXVI. Mountain Army Corps and was promoted to *General der Gebirgstruppe* on 9 November 1944. He saw action in Finland and later in Norway and surrendered to British troops on 9 May 1945. Vogel was sent to the Island Farm Special Camp in January 1946 and was later moved to US captivity from December 1947, finally being released the following year.

Ernst Hermann August <u>Theodor</u> BUSSE
General der Infanterie

* 15 December 1897, Frankfurt an der Oder
+ 21 October 1986, Wallerstein, Bavaria

Knight's Cross: Awarded on 30 January 1944 as *Generalleutnant* and Chief of the General Staff of Army Group South under the leadership of *Generalfeldmarschall* Erich von Manstein for his outstanding achievements during the summer and winter of 1943. From March 1944 he was Chief of the General Staff of Army Group North Ukraine, made up of the 1st and 4th Panzer Armies, while under the command of *Generalfeldmarschall* Walter Model. At the end of July 1944 Busse was appointed Commander of the 121st Infantry Division and took part in the retreat from Leningrad through the Baltic States. In September he was appointed leader of the

Theodor Busse entered Army service with Grenadier Regiment 12 in December 1915 and was commissioned as a *Leutnant* in 1917. He remained in the Army after the war, serving as a legal officer and platoon leader. From July 1937 he was Chief of Operations on the Staff of the 22nd Division with the rank of *Major*. In October 1940 he served as Chief of Operations on the General Staff of the 11th Army, seeing action on the Eastern Front from June 1941.

I. Army Corps and in November he was promoted to *General der Infanterie*. He was officially appointed Commanding General and saw action against the Soviets in the Baltic Sea area near Palangen in Lithuania. On 19 January 1945 Busse was appointed leader of the 9th Army and was soon pushed back from Warsaw to the Oder by the Soviets. In March he received orders to advance south from Frankfurt and together with the 4th Panzer Army was to attack along the Oder. By 22 April Busse and his command were completely surrounded by the Red Army, but the following day he received orders to advance against the eastern flank of the Soviet forces when the 18th and 9th Armies attempted a breakout. Hitler, however, ordered Busse to hold his position at all costs and on 21 April he ordered him to attack Soviet Marshal Konev's armoured forces that had broken through his rear – a completely impossible task as the 9th Army were then having problems retreating. The following day *Generaloberst* Alfred Jodl issued an order, from Hitler's bunker, to Busse for the 9th Army to attack westwards and establish a link with the 12th Army, which only remnants of the Army managed. This included Busse, who surrendered to US forces in May. Busse remained in Allied captivity until 12 December 1947, when he returned to Germany.

Johannes Heinrich Max <u>Gotthard</u> FISCHER
Generalleutnant

* 10 January 1891, Goldap, East Prussia
+ 27 July 1969, Flensburg, Schleswig-Holstein

Knight's Cross: Awarded on 7 February 1944 as *Oberst* and *Führer* of 126th Infantry Division while attached to the XXXVIII. Army Corps for actions in the Soviet Union. On 19 January his division was surrounded by sixty Soviet tanks

Gotthard Fischer joined the Army with Field Artillery Regiment 37 in March 1909 and served as battalion adjutant and later regimental adjutant during the First World War. He left the Army in 1920 with the rank of *Hauptmann*, re-joined in 1936 and was attached to Artillery Regiment 37, now with the rank of *Major*. From July 1938 he was commander of his regiment and took part in the invasion of Poland from September 1939. The following year he saw action in the Battle of France.

and in response he ordered a breakout, which succeeded at around midnight the following night. His troops managed to destroy almost fifty enemy tanks and for this he was awarded the Knight's Cross, it was said that his decision-making saved his division from annihilation and prevented a collapse of the front-line area. Shortly afterwards he was promoted to *Generalmajor* and his command of the division was confirmed. Later his command was pushed back to the west coast of Latvia and in September Fischer was promoted to *Generalleutnant*. On 5 January 1945 he was appointed to Higher Artillery Commander 303 while attached to the 18th Army. By the end of the war he had surrendered to Soviet troops in the Courland area and he remained a prisoner in Russia until 10 October 1955.

Theobald 'Theo' Helmut LIEB
Generalleutnant

* 25 November 1889, Freudenstadt, Württemberg
+ 20 March 1981, Freudenstadt, Baden-Württemberg

Knight's Cross: Awarded on 7 February 1944 as *Generalleutnant* and Leader of the XXXXII. Army Corps as part of the 4th Panzer Army for his skill and leadership in holding the north and north-western front of the Cherkassy Pocket in the Soviet Union. He led with great skill while leading his forces as they pushed their way out of the Soviet encirclement after a ferocious week-long battle with the Red Army.

Knight's Cross with Oakleaves: He became the 400th recipient on 18 February 1944 as *Generalleutnant* and Leader of the XXXXII.

Theobald Lieb entered the Army in March 1910 and served with Grenadier Regiment 123 with the rank of *Leutnant*. He remained in the Army after the war, being promoted to *Major* in February 1932. From November 1938 he was commander of Infantry Regiment 27, seeing action in Poland and later in France as part of the 12th Infantry Division. In October 1940 he served as Commandant of Wuppertal and was promoted to *Generalmajor* in January 1941. From September he took temporary command of the 290th Infantry Regiment. From April 1942 until February 1943 Lieb served as Commandant of Frankfurt am Main.

Theobald Lieb with Hitler at the Wolf's Lair in Rastenburg on 18 February 1944, where he was personally presented with the Knight's Cross with Oakleaves.

Army Corps as part of the 4th Panzer Army, in recognition of his further achievements during the fighting in the Cherkassy Pocket. He showed great skill in the breakout, collecting stragglers from other units, which included the 5th SS-Panzer Division. He led this division, swimming across the Gniloy-Tikich River to safety. For his role in the fighting he became known as the Lion of Cherkassy, and was personally presented with the Oakleaves by Hitler at the Wolf's Lair in Rastenburg on the evening of 20 February 1944. In June Lieb was appointed commander of the 34th Infantry Division and took part in the defensive battles in the Col-de-Ferro, Grimaldi and San Remo areas in Italy. From October he led his troops in the final retreat from Italy and surrendered to American forces on 8 May 1945, remaining in Allied captivity until 1947.

Bernhard Albert <u>Werner</u> RICHTER
Generalleutnant

* 21 October 1893, Zittau, Saxony
+ 3 June 1944, Riga, Latvia

Knight's Cross: Awarded on 7 February 1944 as *Generalleutnant* and Commander of the 263rd Infantry Division, part of the XXXXIII. Army Corps, for actions during the defence of Nevel on the Russian Front from October 1943. He later took part in the retreat from Leningrad and was described by his commanding officer as, 'an excellent commander with experience to become a commanding general'. He continued to see action on the Eastern Front until 21 May 1944, when he was seriously wounded in Latvia, and his commanding

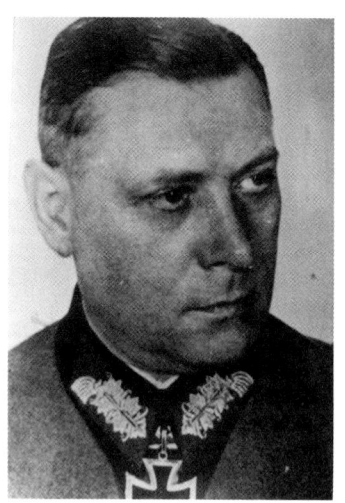

officer, *General der Infanterie* Thomas-Emil von Wickede, described him as 'an active divisional commander who travels a lot with his troops and is calm and confident'. Richter died of his wounds in a hospital in Latvia on 3 June 1944 and is buried in an unknown grave in the German War Cemetery in Riga.

Werner Richter entered Infantry Regiment 12 in February 1912 and later just as the First World War began he served as company leader with the rank of *Leutnant*. He stayed in the Army after the war, rising to the rank of *Major* by February 1932. At the beginning of the Second World War in September 1939 he was serving as Senior Quartermaster of the 4th Army with the rank of *Oberst*.

Karl Friedrich <u>Wilhelm</u> STEMMERMANN
General der Artillerie

* 23 October 1888, Rastatt
+ 18 February 1944 west of Dshurshenzy north Zvenigorodka, Soviet Union

Knight's Cross: Awarded on 7 February 1944 as *General der Artillerie* and Commanding General of the XI. Army Corps for his command accomplishments during fighting south-west of Kremenchuk in central Ukraine as well as his actions in the Cherkassy Pocket in the Soviet Union in January 1944. He led

Wilhelm Stemmermann entered the Foot Artillery Regiment in Karlsruhe in June 1908 and was commissioned as a *Leutnant* the following year. When the First World War began he was serving as adjutant of the II. Battalion with Artillery Regiment 14, being promoted to *Hauptmann* in April 1917. He remained in the Army after the war, rising to the rank of *Oberst* in March 1936 while serving as commander of Artillery Regiment 23 in Potsdam. In October 1937 Stemmermann was appointed Chief of the General Staff of the VIII. Army Corps and in February 1940 he took command of the 296th Infantry Division and saw action in France.

his corps with great skill during late January and early February 1944 during the defensive and bloody battles in Cherkassy, where because of his skill as a commander he was able to save 35,000 men from total defeat and capture by the Soviets.

Knight's Cross with Oakleaves: He became the 399th recipient on 18 February 1944 as *General der Artillerie* and still Commanding General of the XI. Army Corps for his leadership inside the Korsun-Cherkassy Pocket up until the moment of the final breakout. Until that point he had achieved a masterful job of holding the pocket and advancing in the direction of the relief forces. Stemmermann was killed when a Soviet anti-tank shell struck his staff car.

Egbert <u>Georg</u> Sebastian HAUS
Generalmajor

* 16 September 1895, Nuremberg, Bavaria
+ 16 April 1945 near Kaddighagen, East Prussia

Knight's Cross: Awarded on 12 February 1944 as *Oberst* and Commander of Grenadier Regiment 55, part of the 17th Infantry Division, for actions during the heavy fighting around the Lower Dnieper area and in southern Ukraine. Shortly after this he was wounded during action in the Nikopol area and he was hospitalised and entered the Reserves until March 1944. He then took over the leadership of the 17th Infantry Division and on 16 April he was once again wounded and hospitalised. He returned to front-line duty on 7 June as

Georg Haus entered the Army with Bavarian Infantry Regiment 1 from August 1914 and was commissioned as a *Leutnant* the following year, later serving as platoon leader and adjutant. He left the Army in 1920 but returned fourteen years later as an instructor at the War School in Dresden. On 26 August 1939, now with the rank of *Major*, he was adjutant of the 56th Infantry Division and saw action during the invasion of Poland. He was severely wounded with a head shot on 27 May 1940 and did not return to action until October. Haus was regimental commander while attached to the 17th Infantry Division from December 1941 with the rank of *Oberstleutnant*.

leader of the 50th Infantry Division, seeing brief action in the Crimea. From 14 July he attended a divisional leaders course in Hirschberg, returning as commander of the 50th Infantry Division on 29 July. His division suffered heavy losses against the Soviets during the summer offensive and in defensive action in East Prussia, where in October he was promoted to *Generalmajor*. In March 1945 his command was attacked in the Heiligenbeil Pocket and then on 12 April, three days after Königsberg fell to the Red Army where they killed 42,000 Germans and took another 92,000 soldiers prisoner. Four days later, during defensive action near Pillau, about 30 miles west of Königsberg, two German commanders were killed. One was Haus and the other was the commander of the 95th Infantry Division, *Generalmajor* Joachim-Friedrich Lang

<u>Ernst-Anton</u> Fritz Konstantin von KROSIGK
General der Infanterie

* 5 March 1898, Berlin-Potsdam
+ 16 March 1945 near Kandava, Latvia

Knight's Cross: Awarded on 12 February 1944 as *Generalmajor* and Commander of the 1st Infantry Division while attached to the XXXXVI. Panzer Corps in recognition of his outstanding leadership during the fierce battles in the north of Ukraine. His division was particularly active near Berestovka and Stschastliwaja in January 1944 and in the Lypovets Pocket a few days later. He later saw further action in Ukraine when the 1st Panzer Army was encircled between the Bug and the Dnistr Rivers, where from March 1944 his division suffered heavy casualties. Krosigk was promoted to *Generalleutnant* in May 1944 and continued to serve on the Eastern Front until October 1944, when he entered the reserves. On 15 December he was given the leadership of the XVI. Army Corps and saw

Ernst-Anton von Krosigk joined the Army in June 1915 and was commissioned as a *Leutnant* the following year. He saw action during the First World War, serving as adjutant with various units, and remained in the Army after the war. From November 1935 he served with the Army General Staff with the rank of *Hauptmann* and later served as Chief of Operations with the 28th Division. He served as an instructor at the War Academy in Berlin from August 1938 and at the start of the war was Chief of Operations on the General Staff of Army Detachment A. From December 1939 he served as Chief of Operations on the General Staff of the XXII. Army Corps and was promoted to *Oberst* in April 1941.

action in the Courland Pocket, being promoted to *General der Infanterie* on 30 January 1945.

Knight's Cross with Oakleaves: He became the 827th recipient posthumously on 12 April 1945 as *General der Infanterie* and Commanding General of the XVI. Army Corps as part of the 16th Army for his leadership during the defensive attacks against the Soviet 1st Shock Army in February 1945. On 16 March, Krosigk was killed during a Soviet air-attack near Kandava in the Courland area and his body was never found.

Hubertus 'Hubert' LAMEY
Generalmajor

* 30 October 1896, Mannheim, Baden
+ 7 April 1981, Augsburg, Bavaria

Knight's Cross: Awarded on 12 February 1944 as *Oberst* and Leader of the 28th *Jäger* Division while attached to the 16th Army for actions in the Soviet Union. Later in February he attended the 9th Divisional Leaders Course in Hirschberg and then on the 25th he was hospitalised after a skiing accident. He returned to front-line duty on 10 July, when he took over the leadership of the 118th *Jäger* Division when it was sent to guard the Dalmatian coast against possible Allied landings from the Adriatic. On 1 September he was promoted to *Generalmajor* and his command of the division was confirmed. In early 1945 his division was sent to the Eastern Front, where he fought in Hungary and Austria until the end of the war. He surrendered to British troops in Klagenfurt in Austria on 8 May 1945 and he remained in Allied captivity until 30 October 1947, when he returned to Germany.

Dear Reader,

We hope you have enjoyed this book, but why not share your views on social media? You can also follow our pages to see more about our other products: facebook.com/penandswordbooks or follow us on X @penswordbooks

You can also view our products at www.pen-and-sword.co.uk (UK and ROW) or www.penandswordbooks.com (North America).

To keep up to date with our latest releases and online catalogues, please sign up to our newsletter at: www.pen-and-sword.co.uk/newsletter

If you would like a printed catalogue with our latest books, then please email: enquiries@pen-and-sword.co.uk or telephone: 01226 734555 (UK and ROW) or email: uspen-and-sword@casematepublishers.com or telephone: (610) 853-9131 (North America).

We respect your privacy and we will only use personal information to send you information about our products.

Thank you!